C2   1295   780

P9-CAL-807

Chinese Vegetarian Cookery

NOT FOR RESALE
THIS IS A FREE BOOK

BAY AREA FREE BOOK EXCHANGE
10520 San Pablo Ave.
El Cerrito. CA 94530
www.bayareafreebookexchange.com

NOT FOR RESALE
THIS IS A FREE BOOK

BAY AREA FREE BOOK EXCHANGE

WWW.BAYAREAFREEBOOKEXCHANGE.COM

Chinese Vegetarian Cookery

Jack Santa Maria

Illustrated by Kate Simunek

CRCS WELLNESS BOOKS
Distributed in North America by
BOOK PUBLISHING CO.
P.O. Box 99
Summertown, TN 38483
(Telephone: 931-964-3571)

Library of Congress Cataloging-in-Publication Data

Santa Maria, Jack.
    Chinese vegetarian cookery.

    Includes index.
    1. Vegetarian cookery. 2. Cookery, Chinese.
I. Title.
TX837.S256 1987   641.5'636   86-26428

© Jack Santa Maria 1983
Illustrations © Rider & Company 1983

All rights reserved under International and Pan-American Copyright Conven-
tions. Printed in the United States of America. No part of this book may be
used or reproduced in any manner whatsoever (including photocopying)
without written permission from the publisher, except in the case of brief
quotations embodied in critical or scholarly articles and reviews.

FIRST U.S.A EDITION—Originally published in Great Britain
    by Hutchinson Publishing Group

Published in the United States by CRCS Publications

Contents

Introduction

'It is wise to empty the mind and fill the belly,' counselled Lao Zi
(Lao Tsu).* In the ideal country envisaged by the author of the *Dao
De Qing* (*Tao Te Ching*), the people's food was plain and good, just
as their clothes were simple but well made.

In ancient China, the preparation and service of food was an
important part of court ritual, and the first act of many emperors
was to appoint a court chef. As in many other countries, what is
now known as the classic Chinese cuisine was the product of an
affluent Imperial society. This cuisine, which was quite distinct by
the tenth century AD, reached a peak of perfection in the Ching
dynasty (1644–1912). Its best characteristic was an elegant blend of
delicacy and simplicity, and its true elegance was derived from the
cook's ability to reveal the unique qualities of taste, texture and
aroma in each ingredient.

In spite of the counsel given by Lao Zi and Kung Fu Zi (Confucius) in the sixth century BC, while simplicity was the order of the
day among the mass of the people, novelty, ornament and sophistication were pursued by the aristocrats and members of the Imperial
family. Indeed, such elements were often the mark of one's position
in society, and this was as true for the culinary arts as it was for the
design of clothes or noble interiors. This state of affairs was to last
for another 1400 years, yet, as may be seen in the poetry and painting
patronized by the court, the perennial symbol of purity and beauty
was the simple life to be found in the countryside.

The Chinese have traditionally been very aware of the link between diet and health, whether physical, mental or spiritual. Today,
many millions of Chinese are vegetarian by choice, some following
the vegetarian diet preferred by Daoism and later Chan Buddhism,
and the development of soya bean and cereal products has provided
a rich nutritional basis for them. Where meat, poultry or fish are

*All Chinese words are rendered in the internationally recognized Pinyin Romanization.
(See Notes on Chinese Pronunciation and Pinyin Romanization.) Commonly known old-
style renderings of names, books and places are included in brackets.

scarce, many others are vegetarian by necessity. Good, simple cooking based on sound nutritional and economical principles has been encouraged in the People's Republic by the publication of *The People's Recipe Book* (*Dù Zhòng Cài Bǔ*) and by the issue of various other cookbooks by large factories and food corporations around the country.

The traditional recipes in this book are based on the more elaborate restaurant menus available to the traveller as well as on the simple but nutritious cooking to be found in country homes and workers' canteens. They reflect the modern cook's concern to make tasty, attractive and appetizing dishes which are nevertheless nutritionally balanced (containing wholefoods wherever possible), economical and with the minimum of waste.

China (*Zhōng Guó*), the Middle Country, is the third largest country after the Soviet Union and Canada. This great landmass of deserts, plains, lakes and mountain ranges is open on its eastern and south-eastern boundaries to the Yellow Sea (*Huáng Hǎi*), the East China Sea (*Dōng Hǎi*), and the South China Sea (*Nán Hǎi*). Like India, the sheer size of the country, providing contrasts in climate and geography, has given rise to many different styles of cookery. Every region is well known for particular dishes, although four main styles may be distinguished today.

The outline of the written Chinese character for 'country' is a square, almost like the outline of China itself. If this square is divided into three horizontal bands, a rough plan of the culinary regions results. The Northern style includes the cuisine of the capital Beijing (Peking), Mongolia and the northern provinces. The middle band divides into two parts giving the Central Western style of Sichuan and Hunan provinces, and the Central Eastern style of Shanghai. The Southern style is centred on Guangzhou (Canton) and the southern provinces. The visitor to China today will be able to find good restaurants in the main towns which reflect all these styles.

The Northern style has evolved from a meeting of many traditions. It is an oilier, saltier and spicier cuisine than in the south, and dumplings, buns and noodles, rather than rice, are the staple foods. In these northern provinces, which suffer extremes of temperature and biting winds in winter, the food must provide heat and insulation, and this is supplied by the use of spices and a variety of wheat flour products. The Muslim cooking of the tribes of Mongolia and Xinjiang has contributed the techniques of barbecuing, boiling and the use of rich seasonings and sauces, and the Mongol rule in the thirteenth and fourteenth centuries ensured that these features became part of the cuisine of the capital Beijing. Finally, under the influence of the last dynasty – the Manchu – the cuisine of the old Imperial Palace produced the Manchurian element of rarity and sophistication.

The Central Western style of Sichuan and Hunan provinces is less oily and more chilli-hot than the Northern style. It is said that the constant drizzle and fogs of Hunan made that region famous for its hot spicy dishes, but it is just as likely that the climate has made it ideal chilli-growing country. The style is noted for hot spicy food with peanut sauce; cold noodles in red pepper and sesame oil; minced bean curd with chilli-cooked vegetables; and sliced vegetables cooked in a sauce known as 'fishy flavour'. This sauce is made from a combination of garlic, vinegar, ginger and chilli, and has nothing to do with fish!

The Central Eastern style is based on the cities of Shanghai, Nanjing, Suzhou and Hangzhou. The cuisine usually takes a little longer to cook, the vegetables consequently tending to be softer and thus absorbing more of the sauces. Shanghai dishes are delicately flavoured, seasonings tend to be sweet rather than hot and more sugar and dark soy sauce are used. Noodles as well as rice are popular as in the Southern style. Favourite cooking techniques are the 'red-cook' and 'sweet-and-sour' methods. Much thought is given to the appearance of a dish; vegetables, bean curd and other food items are often carefully shaped into the forms of little animals and flowers, in designs to please the eye.

The Southern style is centred on Guangzhou (Canton), the capital city of the subtropical Guangdong province and the most important industrial and foreign trade centre in south China. Situated on the northern edge of the Pearl River delta, Guangzhou has retained its distinctive nine-tone dialect (Cantonese), and its own literature, arts and music. Because Cantonese chefs have gone to live all over the world, the cuisine is probably the most familiar style known to the West and most of the Chinese restaurants outside China are of this type. The chefs have often had to turn to other local ingredients to create their Cantonese dishes abroad so that many of them hardly resemble the Guangzhou originals. However, this ability and enthusiasm to use whichever ingredients are to hand is part of the Chinese character and thus part of its evolving culinary repertoire. I will always remember the story of a friend whose Chinese wife had just arrived in England. When he returned home one evening, he found that she had been out during the day picking fern tops and other spring shoots on a nearby heath which she gently cooked and then carefully presented as part of the evening meal.

Features of the Guangzhou style are its great variety, the delicacy and sweetness of its flavour and the beauty of its presentation. Steam and water are used more than oil, and the abundant vegetables of the region are cooked for the shortest possible time to retain their natural crispness. Typical cooking techniques are steaming and stir-frying. In the former, food is often first marinated in wine or a sweet sauce, then steamed until tender. Stir-frying is done with the oil very hot so that the food crackles and sizzles as it quickly cooks.

Apart from the climatic conditions which determine the availability of plants and spices, other environmental conditions have affected the style of Chinese cuisine. With only seven per cent of the land being suitable for farming, most of it is devoted to cultivation so that few dairy products are produced. Rice, wheat and millet are the most widely cultivated grains and the protein-rich soya bean the most cultivated legume. However, sweet potatoes are second only to rice in the tonnage they yield. Although Kung Fu Zi (Confucius) advised that a meal would be a poor one unless accompanied by polished rice, this is still very much a luxury in many parts of the country.

In some regions the chronic shortage of fuel for cooking has produced the need for techniques ensuring maximum fuel economy. By cutting food into small pieces, it can be cooked by stir-frying on a hot flame for only a few minutes. Not only does this use a minimum amount of fuel, but the vitamin-rich vegetable juices are sealed in. Steaming, the other common Chinese cooking technique, also depends on minimum fuel and maintains food quality through the gentleness of the method. Even today, few Chinese kitchens have ovens for baking or roasting. These typical Chinese techniques may also be the natural outcome of applying religious and philosophical concepts to cookery.

Philosophy and religion, crystallizing as Daoism during the Zhou dynasty of the sixth century BC, encouraged a person to seek union with natural law, to live a simple, balanced life and to eat a predominately vegetarian diet. Such ideas seem to have been part of the Chinese view of life for many centuries. They can be found in the wisdom of the *Yi Qing* (*I Ching*), the origins of which seem to reach back to the writing of the first Chinese books. In the middle of this book of divinatory readings is the hexagram known as 'Jaws', signifying 'Nourishment'. Notice how people nourish others, says the text, and then notice what sorts of things they like to nourish themselves with; such observation will tell us much about their characters. The wise person is thoughtful in speech and frugal in his eating and drinking, the reading counsels.

Daoism teaches that the universe exists by virtue of the tension or balance between two complementary but interdependent forces in matter. These forces, known as Yin and Yang (the negative and positive principles in nature), are mentioned in an appendix to the

Yi Qing, the 'Xi Zi' (fourth century BC). They are often symbolized by pairs of apparent opposites such as dark and light, female and male, moon and sun, soft and hard, and so on, and it is the balancing of these forces that brings about a state of harmony. Assuming that happiness was the natural state of being, Chinese thought has, from ancient times, sought to bring about this state of harmony in every sphere of life. Later, the middle-way teachings of Buddhism (first century AD) reinforced this approach. The Buddhists also brought with them from India the code of *ahimsa* (non-injury) which advocated a vegetarian diet.

These principles can be seen in Chinese cookery today. The ingredients are as fresh as possible, clean and carefully chosen, and then carefully prepared. Each dish must show a harmonious balance of taste, texture, colour, aroma and quality. The five tastes of salt, sweet, sour, hot and pungent must be present. Texture must vary so that the whole meal contains dryness, smoothness, crispness, juiciness and softness. Where possible, the meal as a whole should also reflect this harmony so that the dishes complement each other in their content and in the order in which they are served.

Perhaps it is more than coincidence that the ancient land which thought of itself as the centre or middle of the earth should have given to world cookery the wisdom of balance and harmony in all things. In the complete experience of Chinese food we find the blending of culinary science (the cooking) with culinary philosophy (the choice of ingredients) and the culinary art (the preparation, arrangement and presentation).

This book is for you, the cook who seeks to create in your own kitchen that magical blend of the five flavours, the five textures, the five harmonies and the five criteria of deliciousness. Creation implies rearranging the balance of Yin and Yang. In doing so, you will discover the five culinary adventures!

Preparation and Utensils

If you want good food, cook it yourself.
TRADITIONAL CHINESE SAYING

Since Chinese cookery is concerned with the principles of harmony, the best results will be obtained if you are feeling harmonious and at one with the world. The Chinese sages advise us not to prepare food if we are feeling sick or bad tempered.

Ingredients should be as pure and as fresh as possible. Vegetables and fruit should be carefully washed and carefully prepared. Dishes should be chosen so that they provide a balance and variety in ingredients and cooking methods. Wholefoods are preferred in Chinese cookery. There is no need to use chemical additives in an attempt to make the food more attractive or delicious since this would contradict the aim of the cook to provide food in as pure a form as possible. Chinese cooking techniques are designed to expose the intrinsic deliciousness of any food, and perhaps to complement it, but never to mask it.

No special equipment is needed for Chinese cookery, although a good sharp cutting knife is essential. Cutting vegetables with a small cleaver will speed up cutting time. This way of chopping food is preferred by many cooks and only requires a little practice to produce good results. Relax and aim at producing a light chopping rhythm. It is this relaxed rhythm which gives even chopping. Thickness of slice is then governed by the speed at which you gently nudge the vegetable towards the blade. Frying may be done in a frying pan or a *chǎo guō* (*wok* in Cantonese).* The wok is a large bowl-shaped frying pan with a wooden handle. This inexpensive pan is very easy to manipulate and it is the perfect pan for most of your Chinese cookery; you will find it a joy to use. Steamers may be improvised by the use of pans and colanders, but if you like

*Since the Cantonese term has now become part of the language, the word *wok* will be used to refer to the Chinese frying pan.

steamed food it is well worth purchasing a Chinese bamboo steamer which is pleasant to handle and to look at. A selection of ladles, spoons and strainers will come in handy. As with all kitchen equipment, buy the best that you can afford.

Cutting the ingredients into uniform sizes for use in the same dish ensures even cooking. For stir-frying (*chǎo*), vegetables are usually sliced (*piàn*), shredded (*sī*), diced (*dīng*) or cut into strips or chips (*tiáo*). Some dishes will indicate by their Chinese names how the vegetables are to be cut: for example, in the dish Fried Aubergine (*Zhá Qiézi Piàn*), the aubergine is sliced. You can also estimate the time needed to cook a dish by the way in which the ingredients are cut. The smaller and thinner the pieces, the faster will the dish be to prepare – sometimes only a matter of minutes – and fast cooking preserves the flavour and texture of the vegetable. Stewing or steaming produces the quality of softness as well as juiciness. These slower processes also enable flavours to become more mixed, or the vegetable may be enhanced by the flavour of a herb or spice.

If the vegetable needs to be sliced, cut it diagonally across the grain. All other cutting follows from the process of cutting into sections or chunks (*kuài*). Cut along the grain of each section to form rectangular pieces; these pieces can then either be cut into strips or slivers, and the strip or chip can also be diced. The slivers can be sliced again to form thinner strips or shreds. Thin slices can, of course, be made into strips or shreds in the same way.

Get to know your vegetables. A knowledge of how they are formed will enable you to make the most attractive cutting for the purpose in hand.

Chinese cookery is simple and rewarding, and a few hints will ensure your success. Prepare your cold food and do any baking well in advance. If you can, do your soaking or marinating the day before. Since most cooking methods are done very quickly, it is essential to complete all the cutting and chopping before you begin as the stir-fried meal must be cooked in a matter of minutes. Have your guests sitting at the table; while they are chatting, turn up the heat under your wok, put in the oil and, as soon as it is hot, start cooking the ingredients in the order given in the recipes, keeping your spoon or slice moving all the time, turning and mixing. No sooner than the appetizing aroma of the food has reached your guests then you have arrived with the steaming hot bowls.

Serving and Chopsticks

Don't give yourself away for a piece of food.
WU CHENG EN, *Monkey*

Chinese food can be presented without acquiring any special plates or cutlery. However, the addition of a few items to your cupboard will give a more authentic feel. Each person will need a dinner plate, a bowl for rice and soup, a porcelain spoon for drinking the soup and a pair of chopsticks (*kuàizi*) for eating the solid food. Plates and bowls with pleasing colours and designs go very well with Chinese food. All the dishes of the meal can be placed on the table at the same time or they may be brought in batches in an order which the cook has decided is the most interesting and harmonious, and each person helps himself in any order. If you are not sure how much food to prepare, a good guide is to allow one dish per person. This will allow plenty for all with some left over for the unexpected. Soup should be available to wash down the main course, and a refreshing drink of tea without milk or sugar is usually served at the end of the meal.

According to the number of people who are going to eat together, the Chinese prefer to increase the number rather than the quantity of the dishes to be prepared. It is easier on the cook if a proportion of the dishes can be prepared in advance. A meal of nothing but stir-fried dishes, apart from being unbalanced from the point of technique, means a lot of time spent in the kitchen at the last moment.

In the days of the Imperial past, banquets with eighty or a hundred dishes were common. Today, a banquet will probably have no more than ten, but the ritual of eating will be very similar. Guests are greeted with cups of special teas or juices and little bowls or plates of appetizers such as lotus nuts, dried lichees, honeyed dates and crystallized fruits flavoured with ginger or liquorice. Fresh fruits such as melons, pears, grapefruit and fresh lichees may also be available. These appetizers are followed by cold dishes of pickled or specially marinated vegetables and '2000-year-old' eggs, then by a stir-fried dish followed by a thick soup. After this, the more substantial dishes arrive and thin clear soup is available to wash them down. Finally may come sweet dishes, desserts or beautifully garnished, eye-catching plates of sweetmeats. Toasting in wine or lager beer is common and several toasts may be drunk during the course of a meal. In Beijing, toasts may be drunk with *máotái*, a strong spirit distilled from grain.

Chopsticks are used as extensions of the thumb and forefinger in a pincer-like fashion. Either end may be used when stir-frying in a wok, but the thinner blunt end is the eating end. Pick up a chopstick in the hand that you write with and place it in the space between your thumb and forefinger, resting it on the curved middle finger. Place the other chopstick between your forefinger and thumb, keeping the lower chopstick in place. Now use them like a finger and thumb to pick up your food, remembering that the 'thumb' stays in place while the 'finger' moves to grip. With practice, you will soon be able to pick up a few grains of cooked rice. It is said that food should always be raised to the mouth, although in southern China it is common to see the bowl raised to the mouth and the chopsticks used, with the eating ends kept together, like a small shovel. So you can choose the method which you find the easiest or the most attractive. You are now ready to eat like one quarter of the human race does.

The Spices

A truly good physician first finds out the cause of the illness. Having found that out, he first tries to cure it by food. Only when food has failed does he prescribe medication.

SUN SI MO, *Priceless Recipe*, SEVENTH CENTURY AD

It was because of a war between the rich trading cities of Genoa and Venice in 1298 that Europeans first came to know of the fabulous world of spices to be found in the Orient. Only a short while after the Polo family had returned to Venice from their twenty-five-year trip to Asia, Marco Polo was captured in battle and imprisoned in Genoa. To pass away the time of confinement, he dictated his memoirs which included details of the China of Kubla Khan. Apart from the carefully laid-out cities, block printing and paper money, the Polos were fascinated by the vast quantities of spices which were grown and used in China. In the capital city of Dadu (Beijing), they came across the cultivation of ginger and cassia, and rice wines mulled with spices. In the southern city of Hangzhou alone, Marco Polo recorded in his book, *Travels to Tartary and China*, 10,000 pounds of pepper were brought in every day.

Such spices may have been something new for the Italian merchant adventurers, but fifteen centuries before their arrival in China an anonymous poet had written – in *The Great Summons* – about dishes cooked with peppered herbs.

Most spices have pronounced flavours and aromas. In Chinese cookery they should always be used carefully so that the harmony of the dish is preserved.

CHILLI PEPPER (*hóng là jiāo*):The seed pods of *Capsicum annum* or *Capsicum frutescens* which are green or red when fresh; a member of the Solanaceae (nightshade) family which includes the tomato and potato. The seeds are the hottest part of the pepper and they should be removed before the pods are shredded before adding to the food. The seed pods can be preserved by tying in bunches and hanging up to dry. Chilli gives a distinctive flavour to a dish besides making it very hot. Pickled chilli peppers are called *pào là jiāo*. When chilli is fermented with other seasonings, it is *là jiāo jiāng*. Chilli pepper oil is known as *là jiāo yóu* or *là yóu*. To make your own chilli pepper oil (often used in stir-fried dishes), simply use the proportion of one shredded pepper to one tablespoon of oil and cook together gently for five minutes until the oil is dark and well flavoured. Pour the oil off through a strainer.

CINNAMON (*guì*): The dried inner bark of cassia (*Cinnamomum cassia*) is coarser and thicker than true cinnamon (*Cinnamomum zeylanicum*). Because it contains a higher essential oil content, it is more aromatic. Mentioned in the *Chu Su* (fourth century BC), it is one of the oldest known spices. Its name – *guì* – was given to a settlement founded under Qin Shi Huang Di in 214 BC on the Li Jiang river. With its limestone mountain peaks rising from the green plains swathed in mist, Guilin is considered one of China's most beautiful scenic spots. Cinnamon is a digestive and is used in traditional medicine for stomach disorders and for reducing fever. Use small pieces of bark or small amounts of powder.

CLOVES (*dīng xiāng*): The dried fruit of *Myrtus carophyllus* or *Syzygium aromaticum* became the basis of the spice trade. Just as the English word comes from the French *clos*, meaning 'nail', so does the Chinese – 'fragrant nail'. Although the spice has the characteristic appearance of an old-fashioned nail, reference is also found in Chinese literature of the Han period (third century BC) to the 'chicken-tongued spice'. This digestive is also used in traditional medicine as an antiseptic and for toothache.

CORIANDER (*xiāng cài*): *Coriandrum sativum* is an annual plant of the Umbelliferous family which can be grown in the garden. Its fresh leaves are used in the same way as parsley is used in the West, but it has its own distinctive flavour. Also known as *yuán sui*, the dried aromatic seeds are called *yuán sui mǐ*. Wash the leaves and chop.

FENNEL (*huí xiāng*): The small, elongated, pale green seeds of *Foenculum vulgare* taste like aniseed which bears the same name in Chinese. Another member of the Umbelliferae, the seeds are also known as *xiǎo huí*. It is frequently used in modern Chinese herbal medicine, and in ancient China was a remedy for snake-bite.

FIVE-SPICE POWDER (*wǔ xiāng fěn*): A combination of five or sometimes six dried spices. These may be cinnamon, clove, fennel, star anise and the pale Sichuan peppercorn, and may also include nutmeg, cardamom and even ground dried ginger root or orange peel. When used as a condiment for fried food, it is mixed with salt or sea salt and known as *wǔ xiāng yán*. A useful amount of fresh homemade five-spice powder can be made by grinding together a few small pieces of cinnamon, 12 cloves, 2 teaspoons of fennel seed, 2 teaspoons of Sichuan or other peppercorns, with 3 or 4 star anise. Keep the powder in a well-sealed jar in a cool dry place.

GARLIC (*suàn*): *Allium sativum* belongs to the lily family along with onions (*cōng*) and chives (*xiā ye cōng*) and, like them, is a bulbous plant. Each bulb divides into sections known as cloves which should be peeled before use. Garlic loses its strong harsh taste on cooking and becomes aromatic. It is among the oldest known cultivated plants and appears to have been cultivated even before the beginning of recorded history. When purchasing the bulbs, make sure that all the cloves are hard and not discoloured, and keep them in a cool, dry place. Garlic is considered good for health and is said to prolong life.

GINGER (*jiāng*): The dried, spicy, characteristically knobby root of *Zingiber officinalis*. The fresh root is generally preferred to the dried root powder which has a different flavour. It should always be peeled and then finely chopped or sliced, and cooked in hot oil when stir-fried with vegetables. You will know your oil is at the right heat for stir-frying when a slice of ginger bubbles when put into it. If it is added to a dish at a later stage it should be crushed to release the flavour. Ginger also has a long history of cultivation in ancient China; it is mentioned by Confucius (551–479 BC) in his *Analects*. It is used in herbal medicine as a cure for indigestion and colds.

SESAME (*má*): China is the world's largest producer of one of the oldest condiments known to man. The tiny white seeds (*zhī má*) of *Sesamum indicum* are highly nutritious and have a warm, nutty flavour. A favourite taste of the Chinese, the seeds are used whole and also to make oil and sesame seed paste (*zhī má jiāng*).

SICHUAN PEPPER (*huā jiāo*): The dried brown peppercorns of *Xanthoxylum piperitum* have a pungent smell but only a faintly hot taste which brings out the taste of other foods. The peppercorns should be roasted and ground before being used in stir-fried dishes. When mixed with salt to make a condiment for fried food, it is known as *huā jiāo yán*. Like chilli pepper, it can be cooked to make a hot peppery oil (*huā jiāo yóu*). Grind a few peppercorns and add ½ teaspoon of this to 3 tablespoons oil, cooking together gently for 3 or 4 minutes.

STAR ANISE (*dà huí*): *Illicium verum* is a small evergreen tree native to southwestern China and a member of the magnolia (*mù lán*) family. The ripe fruit is hard and brown and opens out into a star-shaped pod, each section of which contains one strong-smelling seed. An essential aromatic oil gives the seeds their distinctive taste which is somewhat like aniseed or liquorice. *Dà huí* is also known as *bā jiǎo*, *dà huí xiāng* and sometimes *huí xiāng*. Like many other cooking spices, it is used as a cure for digestive disorders.

Basic Ingredients

BAMBOO SHOOTS: The easiest way to obtain bamboo shoots is in tins, when they have already been boiled and put in pure water. In this state, they require very little cooking.

BEANS: When dried beans are called for in a recipe, always soak for as long as possible before cooking. If no other protein is included in the meal, try to incorporate a bean or bean curd dish.

BEAN CURD: See notes at the beginning of the Bean Curd chapter.

BEAN PASTE: Sometimes available as 'bean sauce'. Brown bean paste is a mixture of ground lima beans, fermented with malt, flour and salt. Several kinds are available in which spices, chilli or sesame oil are included. In Sichuan, where brown bean sauce originates, the paste is used to season such dishes as Hot Spicy Bean Curd (*Málà Dòufu*). Sweet bean paste or yellow bean sauce is made from fermented soya beans.

BEAN SPROUTS: The nourishing shoot of the widely available mung bean. The Chinese also use soya beans for the same purpose. You can make your own all the year round. Rinse a cup of mung beans and soak in a bowl of water for two days. Spread out on a piece of damp towelling or rag and keep in a warm, dark place, making sure that the beans are kept damp. In a week or so, the shoots will be ready for picking. Use as soon as possible.

CHILLI PEPPER OIL: *Là yóu* is mentioned in the Spices chapter under 'Chilli Pepper'. An acceptable substitute is Red Pepper Oil (*hóng yóu*). Heat 4 tablespoons oil until it is quite hot. Remove the pan from the heat and stir in 3 tablespoons red chilli powder. Once cooked, the oil is ready for use. Red Pepper Oil is excellent as a condiment if you wish to add a hot sauce to your dish.

COOKING OIL: Use soya if possible, with peanut oil as a close second. Any other vegetable oil would substitute.

CORIANDER: Use the fresh green leaves as a garnish in the recipes. Since parsley does not have the same taste, it would be better to substitute with some chopped clover leaf which is nutritious.

CORNFLOUR: Cornflour or cornstarch is used as a thickening agent to turn vegetable juices into sauces. Wheat flour may be substituted but the effect is not exactly similar.

FLOUR: In the recipes, wholemeal or wholewheat flour is preferred for nutritional reasons. Chapati flour is a good substitute. Always make your doughs soft and pliable.

FUNGI: See notes at the beginning of the Fungi chapter.

GREEN ONION: The young or spring onion, known as scallion in Ireland and the United States. The same amount of onion may be substituted in cooking, but use chives as a substitute for garnishes.

PICKLED VEGETABLES: It is common practice in China to pickle vegetables for use during the winter months, and to dry mushrooms for the same purpose. Any type of pickled vegetable that is available may be used when this is called for in the recipes. Take care to adjust the other ingredients so that they harmonize with the taste. It is a good plan to preserve your own favourite vegetables for use with Chinese food.

To do this, here is the basic recipe: Wash and trim vegetables in perfect condition, cutting them up when necessary. Put them in a large earthenware or stoneware pot which has a lid or bung. Add boiled water by the cup until the vegetables are covered by about 3 inches (8 cm) of water. Sprinkle on 1 tablespoon salt for each cup of water used. Seal up the pot with wax or a flour and water paste and leave to stand in a cool place for a minimum of two weeks. You can add other spices to the salt, such as chilli powder, according to taste.

Sichuan preserved vegetable is very salty and spicy, but it can be soaked in water before use if a milder taste is preferred. It may be sliced and used as a pickle, stir-fried with vegetables or bean curd or used as an ingredient in soups.

RICE WINE: Chinese rice wine has its own particular flavour. A good substitute would be dry sherry which is mentioned in the recipes. Keep any good leftover wine for your Chinese cookery.

SALTED BLACK BEANS: Black soya beans fermented with malt, salt and flour are obtained in an almost dry form. They are particularly good for enriching the flavour of a bean curd dish.

SESAME: A favourite ingredient in Chinese cookery. Toast the seeds lightly in a heavy pan before use. Ground sesame seeds are frequently used in the form of a paste. Greek and Middle Eastern stores also sell a sesame paste known as *tahini*.

When a recipe calls for sesame oil, other oils could be used, but sesame oil is characteristic and preferable.

SOY SAUCE: So common as to hardly need introduction. This fermented sauce of soya bean is a highly nutritious, savoury flavouring. Various varieties are on sale, ranging from a thick dark sauce to a lighter thin one.

STOCK: The Chinese try to avoid throwing away food, and developing the stockpot habit is one way of doing this. Make a stock with your leftovers and you will always have an interesting base for a sauce or a soup.

To make a stock, heat 3 tablespoons oil in a stockpan and fry a chopped onion with some chopped green vegetables. Add a cupful of chopped root vegetables such as potatoes, carrots and turnips. Pour on double the volume of water. Drop in a handful of whichever dried peas or beans you have in the house. Season with salt, pepper and soy sauce and bring to the boil. Lower the heat and leave to simmer gently until a rich stock is produced.

Weights and Measures

In Chinese cookery, mastery of the technique and the ability to create a harmonious dish are more important than exact measurements. Simple weights and measures are provided, in Imperial and metric systems, as a starting point for your own experimentation. These may be varied according to taste and necessity.

The cup measure used in this book is one which holds 8 fluid ounces (225 ml) water, 6 ounces (170 g) rice, 4 ounces (100 g) flour.

The teaspoon holds approximately 1/6 fluid ounce (5 ml) and the tablespoon holds approximately ½ fluid ounce (15 ml).

Cup measurements in this book are level. The spoon measurements are as much as the spoon will hold without being heaped. Cup and spoon sizes vary, but you will soon find the amounts which give the result you like best.

The recipes are sufficient for four to six people, bearing in mind the meal guide of one dish per person.

Tales of Mu:
Plain Clothes, Same House

One day Lord Wang, who took an interest in everything, asked his cook, Mu: 'Mu, how did you come to be a cook? I hear that your father was a highly respected carpenter.'

Mu looked up from his chopping board and replied: 'That is so, your honour. My father was indeed a highly respected carpenter. When I was a boy I would watch my father working. The work always proceeded smoothly and quietly. My father's face was calm. He would rejoice at the end of the day when my mother asked him to come for his food. "Now I am in heaven!" he would say. When I was older, I said to my father: "Father, your work is renowned. You are a gifted master carpenter. Rich men pay well for your work. How is it then that you and mother still dress in plain clothes and we still live in this house?" '

'My father did not answer. He just looked at me, smiling.'

'Again I asked: "How is it that mother cooks such delicious food and yet she spends so little on it? I confess, father, my parents are a mystery to me." '

'My father smiled again and put his arm around me. "Just as you will always be a precious mystery to us. My work is beautiful yes. But I am unaffected by the sight of it. It is true that I am so skilful with the plane and the chisel that my work is like music to hear. But I am unaffected by the sound. The finished piece is prized by people of taste. But I am unaffected by whether they consider it good or whether they consider it bad. When I work I am empty." '

' "Is my mother also empty, like you?" I asked.'

'My father nodded and smiled. "Yes. Your mother also is empty – and she knows which part needs to be filled!" '

'I spent some time thinking over my father's words.'

Mu looked down at the chopping board and smoothed it with his hand. He looked back at Lord Wang. 'It was then, your honour, that I decided to be a cook.'

Rice *(Mĭ)*

In many parts of China, except in the northern wheat-producing provinces, cooked rice – *fàn* – is the staple food. It is the bland bulk food, usually prepared very simply, which accompanies the savoury dishes of the meal. To eat a meal *(chī fàn)* is to 'eat cooked rice'. The names of different meals can be expressed in terms of cooked rice: *zǎofàn*, breakfast or 'morning cooked rice'; *wǎnfàn*, supper or 'evening cooked rice'. The *fàntīng* is the dining room of a restaurant or canteen, and the *fànzhuō* is the dining table.

Of all the varieties of rice now available, I have found the long-grained ones the most suitable for Chinese cookery. Glutinous rice is used when its special quality of stickiness is required. If you cannot procure this, cook ordinary rice a little longer until it becomes sticky. Oval-grained rice cooks very well by steaming. Brown rice may be used in any of the ways suggested below. Although the latter takes a little longer to cook, its extra nutritional value makes it an excellent addition to the vegetarian diet.

Plain Boiled Rice *(Mǐfàn)*

I have found the following method both simple and effective. Put on a large pan of water to boil, adding a teaspoon of salt, although this is not always the custom in China. Rice should always be washed and left to soak before use. Put 1½ cups of rice into a smaller pan and fill with water. Stir up the grains and strain off the cloudy water. Do this three times. Fill up again and leave the rice to stand. When the water in the large pan is boiling, place the rice with its soaking water into it. In 11–12 minutes the rice should be ready, the grains tender but firm. Pour into a metal sieve or metal colander, rinse with a little cold water, and leave to drain. Some unnecessary starch is thrown away if you skim the scum from the boiling water and when the rice is finally drained. The drained rice may be kept warm in a gently heated oven. If you like your rice to be sticky enough to form a lump, allow it to boil until this consistency is reached.

Some prefer to put a lid on the pan and let the rice absorb all the water. In this case, an exact amount of water must be added to the rice, and this amount will vary with the type of rice used. Most long-grained rice needs about double the volume of water. Your own experiments will teach you just how much is needed in each case.

Serve each person with an individual bowl of rice.

Plain Steamed Rice *(Zhēngfàn)*

1½ cups oval-grained rice
5 cups water

Wash the rice and drain. Add the clear water and boil for 3 minutes. Make sure that none of the grains are sticking to the pan. Drain and steam for half an hour or until the grains are tender.

This method of cooking rice is common in Changsha, centre of the rice-growing area of China.

Fried Rice *(Chǎofàn)*

4 cups cooked rice	1 cup finely sliced vegetables
3 eggs	½ cup fresh sliced mushrooms
salt and freshly ground pepper for	½ teaspoon fennel seed *or* aniseed
seasoning	1 teaspoon salt
cooking oil	pinch of five-spice powder
½ cup chopped green onions	2 tablespoons soy sauce
1 cup green peas	

Prepare the plain boiled rice and allow to dry thoroughly. Beat the eggs, sprinkling on a pinch of salt and pepper. Heat 2 tablespoons oil in a wok or pan and stir-fry the eggs until they begin to brown a little, stirring them to break up any large lumps. Remove from the pan. Add 2 more tablespoons oil and stir-fry the vegetables and fennel seed for 2 minutes. Add the salt and five-spice powder. Remove from the pan. Put in 2 more tablespoons oil and stir-fry the cooked rice for 2 minutes. Pour on the soy sauce. Now add the cooked vegetables and egg and mix well together. Serve hot.

Unlike most rice dishes, Fried Rice may be served on its own as a tasty snack or meal in its own right. Vegetables which go well with this dish are carrots, green beans, celery, tomatoes and onions.

Fried Rice with Eggs *(Chǎofàn Dàn)*

Prepare fried rice as in the previous recipe, but omit the eggs. Garnish with:

3 hard-boiled eggs, sliced
fresh cucumber, sliced
lettuce shreds

Arrange the fried rice on a serving dish. Put the egg and cucumber slices around the edge and the lettuce shreds on top.

Chopped fresh tomato would add colour contrast. For those who like the taste and aroma of chopped fresh coriander leaf, substitute this for the lettuce shreds.

Rice with Vegetables *(Cài Fàn)*

1½ cups rice	1 cup peas
3 tablespoons cooking oil	1 teaspoon salt
1 onion, finely chopped	1 teaspoon brown sugar
1 teaspoon ginger shreds	½ teaspoon five-spice powder
1 cup sliced green beans	

Wash the rice, soak and leave to drain. Heat the oil in a deep pan and lightly fry the onion for 2 minutes. Add the ginger and fry for a further 1 minute. Add the rice, vegetables, salt and sugar and fry together for 3 more minutes. Pour in 3 cups hot water and bring to the boil. Cover and simmer gently until the rice is cooked. Just before serving stir in the five-spice powder.

Rice with Black Mushrooms *(Dōng Gū Fàn)*

½ cup dried black mushrooms
2 green onions
cooking oil

1 teaspoon soy sauce
½ teaspoon brown sugar
1½ cups rice, washed and drained

The cooking technique is like that of the risotto or pulau. Soak the mushrooms in 2 cups of warm water until they swell and soften. Remove and allow to drain (retaining the water), then slice. Meanwhile chop the onions finely across the stem. Heat 3 tablespoons oil in a deep pan and gently fry the onions. Add the drained mushrooms, soy sauce and sugar. Cook gently until all the juices have evaporated. Add another 2 tablespoons oil and stir in the rice. Cook the rice until the grains become opaque. Make the mushroom water up to 3 cups with water or stock and pour on to the rice. Bring to the boil. Stir the rice. Cover the pan and simmer gently until all the liquid is absorbed (10–15 minutes).

Fresh mushrooms may be used in this dish. Simply wash them, slice and use in the same way, adding 3 cups of water or stock.

Rice Dumplings with Brown Bean Sauce *(Sōngzi)*

2 cups glutinous rice
1 teaspoon salt
4 eggs
large dried bamboo leaves

brown bean paste (see Basic
  Ingredients, p. 24)
five-spice powder

Wash the rice and leave to soak overnight. Drain the next day. Sprinkle on salt, stir in. Put on a pot of water to boil. Hard-boil the eggs. Meanwhile take a bamboo leaf in both hands, folding each end over the other to make a cone shape. You can now hold the cone in one hand with the thumb in front of the two leaf ends and the fingers behind. Fill each cone with about ½ cup rice and a teaspoon of brown bean paste. Fold up the leaf to make a little packet and tie tightly with thin string, thread or raffia. Put the little packets into the boiling water and allow to boil until the rice is well cooked. Remove from the water and allow to cool. The bamboo leaf packets are brought to the table to be unwrapped. Slice the dumplings and the hard-boiled eggs. Arrange together and sprinkle with a little five-spice powder.

If bamboo leaves are not available, aluminium foil could be used as a substitute, but the packet must not be tied too tightly since the rice will expand during the cooking.

Three Kinds of Rice *(Sān Fàn)*

1½ cups rice
cooking oil *or* sesame oil
½ teaspoon fennel seed or aniseed
½ teaspoon sesame seed

seeds from 1 cardamom pod
1 tablespoon cashew nuts
1 tablespoon chopped fresh
   coriander leaf

Boil the rice until it is just cooked and drain. Divide into three equal portions. Heat 1 tablespoon oil and fry the fennel, sesame and cardamom seeds for half a minute. Add the first portion of rice and stir-fry for 1 minute. Remove and keep warm. Heat another table-spoon oil and fry the cashew nuts until they begin to brown. Add the second portion of rice and stir-fry for 1 minute. Remove and keep warm. Sprinkle the coriander leaf over the third portion of rice and mix together. The rice may now be served in three separate bowls or mixed together and served on one dish. Each type of rice will have its own special flavour.

Rice with Beans *(Dòu Fàn)*

1 cup dried beans
1½ cups rice
2 tablespoons cooking oil
1 green onion, chopped

½ teaspoon finely chopped ginger
½ teaspoon salt
pinch of freshly ground pepper
1 tablespoon soy sauce

Boil the beans in slightly salted water until tender. Drain. Wash and soak the rice. Put the rice into a pan of boiling water. Meanwhile heat oil in a wok or pan and stir-fry the green onion and ginger for 1 minute. Add the cooked beans. Stir well so that the beans are covered with the hot oil. Sprinkle on salt, pepper and soy sauce and cook for 2 minutes. When the rice is ready, drain and stir in the fried beans.

Soft Rice (Congee) *(Zhōu)*

Soft rice is made in China in the form of a gruel. It is an excellent pick-me-up after exercise or illness and is easily digested.

Simmer a cup of rice (glutinous rice if available) in 6 cups of water for an hour. This will make a thick gruel which is relished at breakfast time. Various ingredients may be added just before serving, according to taste. These could range from a sprinkling of salt or soy sauce to chilli sauce, slices of omelette or some stir-fried vegetables. Garnish with a spoonful of finely chopped chives, green onion, coriander leaf or watercress.

Brown Rice with Sesame-fried Vegetables *(Chǎo Má Cài Fàn)*

2 cups brown rice
1 teaspoon sea salt
2 green onions
1 cup red radishes
1 carrot
2-inch (5-cm) piece cucumber
3 tablespoons cooking oil

1 teaspoon finely chopped garlic
1 teaspoon sesame seeds
1 tablespoon sesame paste (see Basic Ingredients, p. 26)
soy sauce
lemon juice

Wash the rice three times and boil in plenty of salted water until tender. While the rice is cooking, wash and prepare the vegetables. Slice the green onions finely. Cut each radish in half. Cut the carrot diagonally, then cut each slice in strips. Slice the cucumber (not too thinly), and cut each slice in four. Heat the oil in a wok or pan and stir-fry the garlic for 30 seconds. Add the prepared vegetables and stir-fry for 3 minutes. Add the sesame seeds after 2 minutes. When the rice is tender, drain and stir in the fried vegetables and sesame seeds. Stir in the sesame paste. Sprinkle with a little soy sauce and lemon juice and serve hot with sesame sauce (see recipe for Sesame Sauce) to taste.

Noodles *(Miàn)*

In northern China, wheat products, rather than rice, are the staple food. They take three main forms: noodles, breads and dumplings. Long noodles are served at birthday parties. On those occasions, the cook will not cut them and, when you suck them up, the longer your noodles, the longer will be your happy life.

Boiled Noodles *(Dùn Miàn)*

There are many kinds of dried noodles available and most of them are prepared in the same way. If the packet gives directions on how to cook them, follow these directions. Otherwise proceed as follows:

Bring a pan of water to the boil. Put in about 12 oz (350 g) noodles and simmer for 5 minutes or until the noodles are tender but not sticky. Drain in a sieve or colander, rinse with cold water and serve in a warmed bowl.

Most noodles are delicious served just as they are, but some Chinese like to sprinkle on a little salt, pepper, soy sauce, chilli sauce or sesame oil.

Boiled Noodles with Vegetables (Chǎo Cài Miàn)

12 oz (350 g) dried noodles
3 tablespoons cooking oil
1 teaspoon finely chopped garlic
1 teaspoon finely chopped ginger
2 green onions, chopped
1 cup sliced fresh mushrooms
1 cup chopped spinach or cabbage

1 cup carrot strips
1 teaspoon salt
1 teaspoon brown sugar
2 tablespoons soy sauce
2 tablespoons dry sherry *or* rice wine
1 teaspoon cornflour dissolved in 1
    cup stock

Boil the noodles in slightly salted water until tender. Drain and keep warm. Heat oil in a wok or pan and stir-fry the garlic and ginger for 1 minute. Add the rest of the vegetables and stir-fry for 2 minutes. Add the salt, sugar, soy sauce, sherry, and cornflour mixture and continue cooking until the sauce thickens. Put the noodles on a serving dish and pour the vegetables and sauce on top. Serve hot.

Cold Noodles (Liáng Miàn)

12 oz (350 g) dried noodles
1 tablespoon soya oil or sesame oil

Boil the noodles in plenty of water until tender. They should still have a little bite to them. Drain in a colander and rinse with cold water. Allow to drain. Pour on the oil and mix well into the noodles. They are now ready to serve cold with a sauce (see Sauces, pp. 127–130).

Cold Noodles with Cucumber Sauce (Liáng Miàn Huáng Guā)

cold noodles prepared as above
1 tablespoon sesame oil
1 teaspoon soy sauce
1 teaspoon rice wine *or* dry sherry
1 teaspoon vinegar

1 teaspoon red pepper oil
1 teaspoon brown sugar
½ teaspoon salt
1 cup shredded cucumber
1 hard-boiled egg, sliced

Add the liquid ingredients to the sugar and salt and stir. Mix well and pour over the noodles. Garnish with the cucumber and hard-boiled egg.

Cold Noodles with Red Pepper and Sesame Oils *(Dān Dàn Miàn)*

As the Chinese title suggests, this recipe is only noodles with a sauce, as prepared in Sichuan. It could form the basis of a series of 'only noodles' recipes by varying the sauces.

2 tablespoons sesame paste (tahini)
1 teaspoon finely chopped ginger
1 teaspoon finely chopped garlic
1 tablespoon sesame oil

2 teaspoons red pepper oil
1 tablespoon vinegar *or* rice wine
    or dry sherry
cold noodles, prepared as above

Mix the sauce ingredients together to make a thick sauce. Mix the sauce with the cold noodles. Serve this spicy Sichuan dish with a hot thick soup. An ideal combination to keep out cold winter fogs and drizzle.

Noodles Cooked in Sauce *(Yóu Miàn)*

12 oz (350 g) dried noodles
¾ pint (500 ml) stock
1 green onion, finely chopped
1 tablespoon cooking oil

Boil the noodles in water for 2 minutes only, so that they are softened but only partly cooked. Drain. Now allow the noodles to continue their cooking in simmering stock. While the noodles are cooking, fry the green onion and serve as a garnish.

A more elaborate dish could be made by frying vegetables as in Chow Mien (see below) and adding them to the stock. The noodles can then absorb the taste of the vegetables. By adding more stock, the noodles could be entirely cooked by this method.

Chow Mien *(Chǎo Miàn)*

This dish, as its title suggests, is simply stir-fried vegetables with noodles. Simple, but tasty and nourishing.

12 oz (350 g) dried noodles
6 tablespoons cooking oil
2 green onions, chopped
2 teaspoons finely chopped garlic
2 tablespoons sliced onions
2 tablespoons sliced mushrooms
2 tablespoons celery, sliced
  diagonally
2 tablespoons sliced pickled
  vegetables

2 tablespoons sliced bamboo shoots
2 tomatoes, cut in quarters
2 teaspoons salt
pinch of freshly ground pepper
2 teaspoons brown sugar
2 tablespoons soy sauce
2 tablespoons dry sherry *or* rice wine
1 cup bean sprouts
½ cup finely sliced French or
  runner beans

Boil the noodles in slightly salted water until tender. Drain, rinse and keep warm. Heat the oil and fry the green onion and garlic for 1 minute. Add the rest of the sliced vegetables (except the bean sprouts and French beans) and stir-fry together for 3 minutes. Add the salt, pepper, sugar, soy sauce and sherry, then mix in the noodles and cook together for 3 more minutes. Keep warm. In a small pan, heat a tablespoon of oil and stir-fry the bean sprouts and green beans for 2 minutes. Put the noodles on a serving dish and garnish with the bean sprouts and beans. Serve hot.

You can use your imagination when making Chow Mien. Vary the vegetables according to what is available and use any of the wide variety of dried Chinese noodles. Try other garnishes such as sliced hard-boiled egg, sliced omelette, fried nuts or fresh sliced cucumber.

Canton Fried Noodles *(Chǎo Miàn)*

One of the many versions of Chow Mien, this method of frying noodles is popular in the Guangzhou region of southern China.

6 tablespoons cooking oil
1 lb (450 g) cooked noodles
1 cup sliced mushrooms
1 cup bean sprouts
2 cups stock

½ cup dry wine *or* dry sherry
2 tablespoons soy sauce
1 teaspoon salt
1 tablespoon cornflour dissolved in
  ½ cup water

Heat 3 tablespoons oil. Put the noodles in the pan in one lump and fry until golden on both sides. Transfer to a plate and keep warm. Heat 3 more tablespoons oil and stir-fry the mushrooms and bean sprouts for 2 minutes. Add the stock, dry wine, soy sauce and salt, and simmer. Pour in the cornflour mixture and simmer until the sauce thickens. Pour over the noodles and serve hot.

Spicy Noodles *(Xiāng Miàn)*

12 oz (350 g) dried noodles	1 teaspoon five-spice powder
1 teaspoon finely chopped ginger	1 teaspoon salt
1 teaspoon finely chopped garlic	2 tablespoons sesame oil
2 teaspoons red pepper oil	

Boil the noodles until tender. Meanwhile mix the spices and sesame oil together. Strain the cooked noodles, rinse and mix in the spicy sauce.

These spicy noodles come from Lanzhou and the northern province of Gansu. If you wish to avoid the strong taste of garlic, fry the garlic in a little oil before adding to the noodles or substitute chopped chives or finely sliced green onion.

Crossing-the-Bridge Noodles *(Guò Qiáo Miàn)*

This dish was named during the days of the Imperial court when a bridge divided the Emperor's palace from the rest of Beijing. The cook had to walk from the kitchen, which was outside the walls of the Heavenly City, over the bridge and into the palace, carrying the pot of hot water and noodles. The noodles are said to have been dropped into the pot just as the cook reached the bridge. By the time the pot arrived at the Emperor's table, the noodles were ready for immediate consumption.

Prepare boiled noodles. Serve them with individual bowls of thick soup or sauce to pour over them. In the Shanghai region of eastern China, the act of pouring is known as 'crossing-the-bridge'.

Noodle Soup *(Miàn Tāng)*

2 pints (1 litre) stock	2 tablespoons chopped pickled
1 teaspoon finely chopped ginger	vegetables
2 tablespoons shredded carrot	2 tablespoons sliced mushrooms
2 tablespoons shredded cabbage	4 oz (110 g) dried noodles
stem	salt
2 tablespoons shredded turnip	freshly ground pepper
2 tablespoons bean sprouts	fresh watercress, chopped
2 tablespoons chopped cucumber	

Bring the stock to the boil in a soup pan. Add the ginger and sliced 'hard' vegetables and simmer for 5 minutes. Add the 'soft' vegetables and simmer for a further 2 minutes. Put in the noodles and seasoning to taste and simmer until the noodles are soft. Serve garnished with a little watercress, finely chopped chives or coriander leaf.

Take care to adjust the form of the noodle to this dish, bearing in mind that it is to be eaten as a soup. Break the noodles into small pieces before cooking. Noodles can, of course, be added to many of the soup recipes to add bulk.

Crispy Rice Noodles *(Zhá Mǐ Fěn)*

oil for deep-frying
12 oz (350 g) dried rice noodles
1 green onion, chopped
1 teaspoon finely chopped garlic
1 teaspoon finely chopped ginger
1 cup sliced mushrooms
½ cup cashew nuts

1 cup bean sprouts
1 tablespoon soy sauce
1 teaspoon salt
pinch of freshly ground pepper
1 teaspoon cornflour dissolved in 2 tablespoons stock

Heat the oil in a wok or deep frying pan until very hot. Have a large sieve or draining ladle ready. Put the rice noodles into the hot oil. They puff up and cook immediately so remove with the draining ladle before they overcook. Drain and keep warm. In another pan, pour in 2 tablespoons hot oil and stir-fry the green onion, garlic and ginger for 30 seconds. Add the mushrooms, nuts and bean sprouts and fry for 1 minute. Add the soy sauce, salt, pepper and cornflour mixture. Cook until the sauce thickens, but be careful not to over-cook the bean sprouts. Arrange the noodles like a nest on a serving dish. Pour the mushroom and cashew nut sauce into the centre of the nest. Serve hot.

Breads, Pancakes and Dumplings *(Bǐng)*

Flat Baked Bread *(Miàn Bǐng)*

On the upper reaches of the Yellow River (Huang He) in the Longxi Basin of northwest China, stands Lanzhou, capital of Gansu province. The city is one of the stopping places on the old Silk Road which led westwards from Central Asia to the territories of the Roman Empire. A local speciality is the use of the lily in cooking. The Muslim or Hui community serve flat baked bread with spicy fillings. Here is an adaptation of a typical recipe:

1 cup yogurt
1 cup milk
½ teaspoon baking powder
2 eggs
1 tablespoon cooking oil
6 cups flour

1 teaspoon salt
½ teaspoon ground fennel seed *or* cardamom seed (optional)
1 teaspoon brown sugar
1 tablespoon dried yeast

Beat the yogurt to an even consistency, warm gently in a pan and stir in the milk, baking powder, eggs and oil. Sift together the flour, salt, ground spice, sugar and yeast. Work in the yogurt mixture gradually until a stiff dough is formed. Knead well for at least 15 minutes. Cover with a cloth and leave in a warm place until the dough has risen to nearly twice its original size. Knead again. Break into 8 large balls and, with the help of a little dry flour, shape into flat oval cakes about 10 inches (25 cm) across and of pancake thickness. Brush the tops with warm milk and melted butter or oil. Bake in a hot oven for 10–15 minutes on a greased baking dish. When ready, the breads should be soft and light gold in colour. On special occasions they can be sprinkled with sesame seeds before baking.

When the breads have cooled a little, they can be filled. Make a slit in the side, spread a little bean paste inside and fill with seasoned sliced vegetables such as tomatoes, cucumber, pickles and shredded lettuce. Sprinkle over a little sauce (see Sauces, pp. 127–130) and you have a quick but nourishing meal from northern China. In Lanzhou, these breads are also served with hot spicy noodles.

Sesame Flat Cakes *(Táng Huǒ Shāo)*

As their name in Chinese implies, these fried cakes are sweet to taste. They are, however, an excellent accompaniment to a savoury vegetable dish instead of rice or noodles.

1 teaspoon brown sugar	3 tablespoons sesame paste (tahini)
1½ teaspoons dried yeast	3 tablespoons brown sugar
½ teaspoon salt	1 tablespoon sesame oil
14 oz (400 g) flour	

Put a cup of warm water into a jug and stir in the 1 teaspoon sugar. Add the yeast, and allow to stand for 5 minutes to ferment. In a mixing bowl, sift the salt with the flour and stir in the yeast mixture. Knead well together, adding a little more water to make a soft dough. Cover with a cloth and leave in a warm place to rise for 45 minutes. Preheat the oven to 375°F/190°C/Gas 5. In another bowl, mix together the sesame paste, sugar and oil, blending well. When the dough is ready, knead it again. Divide in 2 portions. Roll out each portion on a floured board to make a thin rectangular sheet. Spread each sheet with half of the sweet sesame paste and roll up, sealing the edge with a little water. Now slice each roll to make 12 circular pieces. Flatten each slice with the palm of the hand. Brush both sides with oil and fry gently in a frying pan until both sides are golden. Put on a greased baking tray and bake for 5–7 minutes. Makes 24.

These nourishing bread cakes are delicious eaten hot and make an ideal teatime snack. Serve with tea, soup, or with pieces of cucumber dipped in salt or a sauce. The recipe is from northern China and is excellent when forming part of a cold weather meal.

To make simple fried cakes *(Shāo Bǐng)* with a more savoury filling, use the following recipe:

Make up the dough as before. Make a spreading paste by mixing 1 teaspoon Sichuan peppercorns and 1 teaspoon fennel seeds, ground together, with 2–3 tablespoons sesame paste (tahini). Spread the spiced paste on the pastry sheets as before and roll up. Slice and press to make flat cakes about 3 inches (8 cm) in diameter. Brush both sides with oil and fry until both sides are golden. Put the flat cakes on a greased baking dish and spread each one with a little honey. Sprinkle with sesame seeds and bake in a medium hot oven for 5–7 minutes.

Crispy Biscuits *(Sū Huǒ Shāo)*

18 oz (500 g) flour
1½ teaspoons salt
2 tablespoons cooking oil
1 tablespoon brown sugar

Sift 13 oz (375 g) of the flour with the salt and gradually add enough water to make a smooth dough. Knead well and leave to stand for 10 minutes. Heat the oil until hot, then rub into the remaining flour, also adding the sugar. Knead together and leave to stand for 10 minutes. Roll out each piece of dough on a floured board, ending up with 2 equal rectangles. Place the oil dough on top of the other piece and roll them up together to make a cylinder. Cut across the cylinder to make circular pieces about 1 inch (2.5 cm) thick. Press each piece gently to flatten to half its thickness. Brush each side with oil and fry in a pan until golden on both sides. Put all the browned biscuits on a greased baking dish and bake for 4–5 minutes in a hot oven. These biscuits are from Beijing.

Fried Bread *(Yóu Bǐng)*

18 oz (500 g) flour
3 teaspoons salt
1 tablespoon baking powder
oil for deep-frying

Sift the flour with the salt and baking powder. Gradually add enough water (about 2 cups) to make a soft dough. Knead well. Cover and leave to stand for 15 minutes. Sprinkle drops of water over the dough and knead again. The dough should be silky smooth. Cover with a damp cloth and leave to stand for 2 hours. Roll out the dough on a floured board to make a sheet about ½ inch (1.5 cm) thick. Cut into rectangles about 8 inches (20 cm) long and 5 inches (12 cm) wide. Make 2 parallel cuts along the surface of each piece, halfway into the dough. Heat the oil in a pan and deep-fry each piece until golden brown. Remove and drain.

In Beijing and the northern provinces, this bread is served in place of rice with stir-fried dishes. It also goes very well with soup.

Fried Bread Twists *(Yóu Tiáo)*

18 oz (500 g) flour
3 teaspoons salt
1 tablespoon baking powder
oil for deep-frying

Sift the flour with the salt and baking powder and gradually add enough water (about 2 cups) to make a soft dough. Knead and leave to stand for 15 minutes. Sprinkle with drops of water and knead again until the dough becomes silky smooth. Cover with a damp cloth and leave for 2 hours. Put the dough on a floured board and pull and roll out to form a ribbon about 2 inches (5 cm) wide and ½ inch (1.5 cm) thick. Cut across the ribbon to make strips about 5 inches (12 cm) long. Wet a strip with a little water and press another strip on top of it. Press down with a rolling pin to make them stick together. Pick up the double strip by the ends, pull gently and twist at the same time. Drop each twist into hot oil and deep-fry until golden. Remove and drain.

These north Chinese breads have the same function as croutons, and are served with soup or soft rice (congee). Break them into pieces and drop into the soup or put a dish of them in the middle of the table with the individual bowls of soup.

Deep-fried Sesame Bread *(Zhá Má Huā)*

2 cups flour
1 teaspoon brown sugar
1 teaspoon salt
1 tablespoon sesame seeds
1 tablespoon sesame oil
oil for deep-frying

Sift the flour with the sugar, salt, sesame seeds and sesame oil. Add enough water (about 1 cup) to make a soft dough. Knead well and roll out on a floured board to make pastry. Cut into strips about 4 inches (10 cm) long. Hold each strip by the ends and give it a twist. Deep-fry the strips in hot oil until golden. Drain and serve hot.

These are very nice to eat with soup or a juicy bean curd dish. The recipe is from Beijing.

Green Onion Cakes *(Cōng Bǐng)*

These cakes are best made in a mould, but if you think of them as small lidded pies about 3 inches (7 cm) in diameter, you will get a similar result.

4 cups flour
1 teaspoon salt
pinch of five-spice powder
4 oz (110 g) margarine
1 egg
1 teaspoon sesame oil

For the filling:
2 tablespoons peanuts
2 tablespoons sesame seeds
2 tablespoons blanched almonds *or* chestnuts, boiled until tender
2 tablespoons walnuts or pine nuts

2 tablespoons cooking oil
5 tablespoons chopped green onion
1 tablespoon finely chopped garlic
½ tablespoon finely chopped ginger
1 tablespoon yellow *or* brown bean paste
½ teaspoon five-spice powder
½ teaspoon salt
2 tablespoons margarine
2 tablespoons rice flour

Sift the flour, salt and five-spice powder together. Cut the margarine into pieces and rub into the flour until it forms crumbs. Add enough hot water (about ½ cup) to make a pastry dough. Cover the pastry with a cloth. Roast the peanuts for 2 minutes in a hot pan. Add the sesame seeds, putting on a lid because the seeds jump, and roast for another 2 minutes. Place the contents of the pan and the other nuts in a grinder or mortar and grind together. Put some cooking oil in the pan and stir-fry the green onion, garlic and ginger for 2 minutes. Add this and the rest of the filling ingredients to the ground nuts and mix well together. Roll out the pastry on a floured board. Cut rounds with a pastry cutter and then make the bowl-shaped base of the pie. Put in a rounded tablespoon of filling, pressing down gently. Wet the edges of the pastry and cover with another round to make a lid. Seal together. Place all the cakes on a greased dish or baking tin. Beat the egg and sesame oil together and brush each cake to glaze. Bake in a hot oven (400°F/200°C/Gas 6) until the cakes are golden brown (about 30 minutes). Makes 16. Serve with a tasty thin soup.

Spicy Pancakes *(Xiāng Bĭng)*

2 cups flour
½ teaspoon salt
2 tablespoons sesame oil

Sift the flour with the salt and rub in the sesame oil. Add enough hot water (just under a cup) to make a soft pliable dough. Knead well and make into a long sausage. Break off pieces the size of ping-pong balls. Flatten with the hand and roll out as thinly as possible. Cook in a pan over a low heat, turning once, until both sides are browned. Serve when a plateful of pancakes is ready. Spread each pancake with sauce, top with filling and roll into a cylinder, tucking in one end as you go.

This recipe from Fujian is an ideal communal meal and a great favourite with guests. The cook has to work hard to make the platefuls of pancakes necessary to keep the guests happy, but you can make some in advance, wrapping them in a damp cloth and keeping them in the gentle heat of the oven. Supply a set of sauces (see Sauces, pp. 127–130) and some dishes of filling. Here are some filling suggestions:

Scrambled eggs: Beat 3 eggs together with 1 teaspoon salt or soy sauce. Stir-fry in 3 tablespoons hot oil.

Fried potatoes: Peel and shred some potatoes. Deep-fry in hot oil until golden.

Peanuts: Toast a cup of peanuts until they begin to brown. Crush the nuts and sprinkle on ½ teaspoon salt and 1 teaspoon oil. Mix well.

Bean sprouts: Put some sprouts in a colander and pour over hot water. Mix with some chopped chives.

Stuffed Pancake Roll (Spring Roll) *(Chūn Juǎn)*

Prepare thin pancakes as in the previous recipe.

For the filling:
3 tablespoons cooking oil
1 egg
½ cup chopped green onions
½ cup sliced mushrooms

2 cups bean sprouts
1 tablespoon soy sauce
pinch of salt and pepper
1 tablespoon bean paste (see Basic
    Ingredients, p. 24)

Heat a tablespoon oil in a pan. Break in the egg and stir-fry until well cooked. Remove and keep the egg to one side. Heat 2 more tablespoons oil and stir-fry the green onions and mushrooms for 30 seconds. Add the bean sprouts, soy sauce, salt and pepper and mix well for a further 30 seconds. Remove from the heat. Stir in the egg and bean paste and mix well. Put some filling on a pancake. Fold in the sides. Roll up and wet the edge with water before sealing. Deep-fry in hot oil until golden. Serve hot. Keep crisp in the oven.

As with all the filling recipes, this one may be used as a guide. Use your own imagination to create your own tasty fillings. The accent may be on spiciness, chilli hotness or sourness, but try to include the textures of crunchiness and juicy tenderness as found in bean sprouts and mushrooms.

Bean Paste Pancakes *(Jiàng Bǐng)*

Prepare pancakes as in the recipe for Spicy Pancakes.

celery
cucumber
carrot
bean paste mixture (see Basic
  Ingredients, p. 24)

Wash the vegetables and prepare for cutting. Cut along the length of the vegetables to form long strips. Spread each pancake with bean paste mixture. Put in strips of raw vegetables as desired and roll up to eat.

Thin Pancakes *(Bāo Bǐng)*

12 oz (350 g) flour
1 teaspoon salt
cooking oil

Sift the flour with the salt and add enough hot water (about 1½ cups) to make a soft dough. Divide into 24 small balls. Flatten each ball until it is about 2 inches (5 cm) in diameter. Brush the top of one round with oil and put another over it. Roll together with a rolling pin to make a pancake about 6 inches (15 cm) in diameter. Heat a heavy pan and bake each pancake on both sides. Keep the cooked pancakes wrapped in a cloth on a warmed dish. When ready to be eaten, peel each pancake into two (the oil layer allows them to separate).

These wheat pancakes, somewhat like Indian chapatis, are a favourite in Beijing. Serve with a dish of bean sprouts, stir-fried eggs or sliced omelette, and individual bowls of plain soup or soft rice (congee). Put a little of the bean sprouts and eggs on the pancake. Fold over one end and roll up. You can now bite the juicy open end. Wash down with sips of rice soup.

Steamed Vegetable Buns *(Bāozi)*

3 teaspoons dried yeast
1 teaspoon brown sugar
1 lb (450 g) flour
2 tablespoons cooking oil
2 tablespoons finely chopped green onions
1 teaspoon finely chopped ginger

9 oz (250 g) chopped mixed vegetables
½ teaspoon sesame seeds
2 tablespoons soy sauce
2 tablespoons dry sherry *or* rice wine
½ teaspoon salt

Sprinkle the yeast on to a cup of lukewarm water in a jug. Add the sugar and stir. Leave to stand for the liquid to double its size. Put the flour in a bowl and stir in the yeast mixture. Add warm water (1–1½ cups) gradually to make a nice elastic dough. Knead well, cover with a cloth and leave to rise for an hour in a warm place. Heat the oil in a wok or pan and stir-fry the green onions and ginger for 30 seconds. Now add the vegetables and sesame seeds and stir-fry for a further 30 seconds. Remove from the heat and mix in the soy sauce, sherry and salt. This is the filling mixture.

When the dough has doubled its size, knead it again for a few minutes and roll out on a floured board to make a long sausage about 2 fingers in diameter. Cut the sausage into rounds about 1 finger in thickness. Flatten each round with the palm of your hand and roll out to make a small pancake. Put a tablespoon of the filling in the centre. Gather the edges of the pancake and pinch them together at the top with a little twist. This will create characteristic pleats at the sides of the little dumpling. Put the dumplings on damp muslin, waxed paper or foil on a rack in a steamer and steam over a high heat for 10 minutes. Serve hot.

Bāozi are very popular in Beijing and the north of the country. Leftover fried rice would also make a good filling for the dumplings. This is a very good recipe to make with the family or a group of friends – each one in charge of part of the process.

Vegetable Dumplings *(Jiăozi)*

2 cups flour	1 green onion, finely chopped
½ teaspoon salt	2 tablespoons soy sauce
1 cup chopped spinach	1 teaspoon brown sugar
½ cup chopped leeks	½ teaspoon salt
½ cup bean sprouts	1 tablespoon sesame oil

These dumplings are rather like the steamed buns of the previous recipe except that the dough is made without yeast and is rolled out thinly. Sift the flour with the salt and add enough water (about 1 cup) to make a nice silky dough. Knead well and cover with a cloth. Prepare the filling by mixing the rest of the ingredients together in a bowl. Knead the dough again and break into walnut-sized balls. Flatten and roll out to make a thin pancake. Put ½ tablespoon of filling in one half of the pancake. Wet the edge with water, fold over and press together to make a half-moon-shaped dumpling. Place in a steamer and cook for 10 minutes on a high heat or boil in water for the same length of time. Serve dipped in a mixture of vinegar and soy sauce.

Another way to prepare these Beijing dumplings is to deep-fry them in hot oil until the pastry is golden.

Bean Curd *(Dòufu)*

This white, almost tasteless and odourless substance, with a texture somewhat firmer than blancmange, is fast becoming one of the most important foods of the late twentieth century. The West has discovered the versatile soya bean, with its protein content equivalent to that of the finest steak. Although it may now become the answer to the world's shortage of protein food, it has been known to the Chinese for thousands of years.

If soya beans are crushed, boiled in water and strained, and the resulting paste pressed in a mould, the product is known as bean curd *(dòufu)*. Bean curd is low in calories and is cholesterol free. In its soft form, it can be used in place of milk products in such things as cakes and ice cream. Bean curd can be fried and dried. It can be used as a protein base for soups and vegetable dishes or it can be specially cooked and spiced to take its own place in the meal. In fact, it is the ideal food for vegetarians.

Bean curd can be purchased in packets of dried strips ready for use. Simply soak the strips in water until they are soft. When purchasing soft bean curd, make sure that it is absolutely fresh and in water which should cover it entirely. Keep it in a cool place and, like milk, use it as soon as possible. One piece makes four cakes.

If you want to make your own fresh bean curd sheets (*dòufu yī*), grind soaked soya beans to make a white liquid – soy milk. Boil the milk until a thin skin is formed on the surface. This process is rather like the formation of a skin of cream on the top of boiled milk. The soy milk skin can be picked up with chopsticks or a slice, and dried. Fresh *dòufu yī* can then be fried and served with sweet-and-sour sauce or a vegetable dish.

Pressed bean curd (*dòufu gān*) is a firmer form of the curd and one of the major ingredients in Chinese vegetarian cookery. Various kinds are found in China: when seasoned with spices and soy sauce, it is known as 'fragrant dry bean curd' (*xiāng dòufu gān*). It can be shredded and used straight away in salads or cold food, or stir-fried with vegetables. When pressed bean curd is unobtainable, use fried bean curd instead.

Fried Bean Curd *(Zhá Dòufu)*

2 cakes bean curd, drained	1 tablespoon dry sherry *or* rice wine
3 tablespoons cooking oil	1 teaspoon red pepper oil
4 tablespoons soy sauce	2 tablespoons finely chopped
2 tablespoons vinegar	coriander leaf

Slice the cakes in half, then cut the four halves into triangular pieces. Heat the oil in a wok or pan and fry the bean curd until golden. Stir the sauce ingredients together in a bowl and serve the bean curd with the sauce poured over it.

Fried Bean Curd with Cabbage *(Chǎo Dòufu Xīncài)*

1 lb (450 g) cabbage	1 cup stock *or* water
cooking oil	2 cakes bean curd, chopped
2 teaspoons salt	1 cup sliced bamboo shoots
1 tablespoon soy sauce	2 tablespoons dry sherry *or* rice wine

Wash the cabbage and cut the leaves from the central stem. Cut the leaves into small square pieces. If the stem is not too tough, cut it into thin slices. Heat 3 tablespoons oil in a wok or pan and stir-fry the cabbage until it begins to soften. Add the salt, soy sauce and stock. Cover and simmer gently for 4 minutes. In another pan, stir-fry the bean curd and bamboo shoots in 3 tablespoons oil for 3 minutes. Add the sherry. Mix with the cabbage and serve hot.

This style of bean curd is from Suzhou in Jiangsu province.

Sichuan-style Bean Curd *(Má Là Dòufu)*

4 cakes bean curd	2 dried red chillis
2 green peppers	1 tablespoon soy sauce
1 leek	1 tablespoon dry sherry *or* rice wine
2 green chillis	2 tablespoons yellow bean paste
3 tablespoons cooking oil	2 teaspoons sesame oil

Slice each cake of bean curd and cut each slice diagonally to form 2 triangles. Wash the vegetables. Cut the peppers in half, take out the seeds and slice into strips. Slice the leek diagonally. Slit open the green chillis and take out the seeds; slice. Heat the oil in a wok or pan and fry the bean curd for 2 minutes. Remove and drain. Add a little more oil if necessary and stir-fry the vegetables and red chillis for 2 minutes. Add the soy sauce, sherry and yellow bean paste. Mix well, add the bean curd and stir together for 2 minutes. Sprinkle on the sesame oil and serve hot with boiled rice.

Bean Curd in Brown Bean Sauce *(Yúxiāng Dòufu Sī)*

This spicy dish is said to imitate 'fish flavour' although it does this in name only.

2 cakes bean curd	1 teaspoon finely chopped garlic
1 tablespoon dry sherry *or* rice wine	1 tablespoon brown bean paste
1 tablespoon soy sauce	1 tablespoon vinegar
1 teaspoon cornflour dissolved in 1 tablespoon water	1 teaspoon salt
	1 teaspoon brown sugar
4 tablespoons cooking oil	1 teaspoon chilli pepper oil
1 teaspoon finely chopped ginger	1 teaspoon sesame oil

Drain the bean curd and sliver. Marinate in a mixture of sherry, soy sauce and cornflour water for a few hours. Heat the oil in a wok or pan. Strain the bean curd but keep the marinade. Fry the bean curd until golden. Add the marinade and the rest of the ingredients. Mix well and cook together for 3 minutes. Serve hot.

Bean Curd in Yellow Bean Sauce
(Zhá Dòufu Miàn Jì Jiàng)

4 cakes bean curd
pinch of five-spice powder
4 tablespoons soy sauce
cornflour
cooking oil for deep-frying
1 tablespoon brown sugar

3 tablespoons yellow bean paste
cucumber, sliced and cut in
  quarters
green onions or chives, finely
  chopped

Cut the bean curd into small cubes. Stir the five-spice powder into the soy sauce, then mix this with the bean curd and allow to stand for 1 hour. Remove the curd from the marinade and roll each cube in cornflour. Heat the oil in a wok or deep pan and deep-fry the cubes until they begin to turn golden. Remove and drain. Mix the sugar with the yellow bean paste. Heat a tablespoon oil in another pan and stir in the sauce. Stir together over the heat until the sauce begins to bubble. Add the bean curd cubes and roll in the sauce until they are well coated. Put on a serving dish and garnish with the cucumber and green onion. Serve with boiled rice or noodles.

Bean Curd Slivers *(Dòufu Sī)*

4 cakes pressed bean curd
3 tablespoons soy sauce
2 tablespoons dry sherry *or* rice
  wine

3 teaspoons brown sugar
2 teaspoons sesame oil

Sliver the pressed bean curd. Place in a pot and fill with boiling water. Allow to cool and pour off the cloudy liquid. (This is full of starch and is not worth keeping for stock.) Combine the rest of the ingredients and mix well until the sugar is dissolved. Pour boiling water over the slivers again and drain. Put the slivers on a serving dish and pour over the sauce. Mix gently and serve with rice or breads and a vegetable dish.

Bean Curd in Sweet Sauce
(Dòufusī Tángyóu)

bean curd slivers prepared as in the
  recipe above
1 tablespoon brown sugar
3 tablespoons warm water

1 tablespoon dry sherry *or* rice wine
2 teaspoons sesame oil
2 teaspoons sesame seeds

Scald the bean curd slivers and allow to drain. Combine the rest of the ingredients for the sauce mixture and pour this over the bean curd. Serve with rice and sweet-and-sour or sour vegetables.

Bean Curd in Vegetable Sauce *(Dòufusī Càiyóu)*

bean curd slivers prepared as in the
  Bean Curd Slivers recipe
2 cups vegetable stock
1 teaspoon brown sugar

2 teaspoons sesame oil
1 teaspoon bean paste (see Basic
  Ingredients, p. 24)

Scald the bean curd slivers with boiling water and allow to drain. Combine the rest of the ingredients for the sauce. Heat gently and put in the slivers. Heat for 2 minutes and serve. A teaspoon of cornflour dissolved in 1 tablespoon water may be added to thicken the sauce. Serve hot with fried rice and bean sprouts.

Bean Curd with Turnips *(Dòufu Lóbō)*

1 tablespoon salted black beans
½ lb (225 g) turnip, washed and
  peeled
3 tablespoons cooking oil
2 green onions, finely chopped
1 teaspoon finely chopped garlic

1 teaspoon finely chopped ginger
1 teaspoon sesame seeds
2 tablespoons soy sauce
1 tablespoon dry sherry *or* rice wine
1 teaspoon brown sugar
2 cakes bean curd, chopped

Wash the salted beans in a colander or sieve and leave to drain. Cut the turnip into thin slices across the root, then cut each slice into strips. Heat the oil in a wok or pan and fry the green onion and garlic, ginger and sesame seeds for 30 seconds. Add the beans, turnip, soy sauce, sherry and sugar and stir together for 2 minutes. Gently stir in the bean curd and cook together until the turnip is tender. Serve hot with rice. Other roots such as swede, parsnip or radish may be substituted or mixed together to make this tasty bean curd dish.

Chopped Bean Curd with Spinach
(Dòufu Bócài)

3 tablespoons cooking oil
2 cakes bean curd, chopped
1 cup chopped leek
2 cups chopped spinach

1 tablespoon dry sherry *or* rice wine
1 tablespoon soy sauce
1 tablespoon yellow bean paste
1 tablespoon sesame oil

Heat 2 tablespoons cooking oil in a wok or pan until hot and fry the bean curd for 2 minutes. Remove from the pan. Add another tablespoon oil and fry the leek and spinach for 2 minutes. Stir in the sherry, soy sauce and yellow bean paste. Carefully add the bean curd and cook together for 2–3 minutes. Pour on the sesame oil and serve hot with rice or noodles. Red chillis or peppers may be added for those who like this dish hot.

Chopped Bean Curd with Assorted Vegetables
(Shí Jǐn Dòufu)

1 lb (450 g) vegetables, sliced
4 tablespoons cooking oil
2 cakes bean curd, chopped
½ onion, cut across then sliced
1 teaspoon finely chopped garlic
2 tablespoons soy sauce
1 tablespoon dry sherry *or* rice wine

½ cup stock
1 teaspoon brown sugar
1 teaspoon salt
1 teaspoon cornflour dissolved in 1
   tablespoon water
2 teaspoons sesame seeds, toasted

Wash and prepare the vegetables, cutting them into small pleasing shapes. Heat 2 tablespoons oil in a wok or pan and stir-fry the bean curd for 2 minutes. Remove from the pan. Add 2 more tablespoons oil and fry the onion and garlic for 30 seconds. Now add the vegetables and fry for 2 minutes. Stir in the sauce ingredients and carefully add the bean curd. Cook until the sauce thickens. Serve sprinkled with sesame seeds.

The vegetables should be chosen for contrast in colour, taste and texture. Cut leeks and carrots diagonally. Cut big roots into strips. Slice bamboo shoots, red radishes and green beans. Break up cauliflowers into small florets. Chop greens.

Hot Spicy Bean Curd *(Má Là Dòufu)*

2 tablespoons cooking oil
2 green onions, chopped
1 teaspoon finely chopped garlic
1 or more green chillis, seeded and
  chopped
1 tablespoon salted black beans

2 bean curd cakes, cut in cubes
1 tablespoon soy sauce
1 teaspoon brown sugar
½ cup stock
1 teaspoon cornflour dissolved in 1
  tablespoon water

Heat oil in a wok or pan and fry the green onion, garlic and chilli for 30 seconds. Add the salted beans and bean curd cubes and fry gently until the bean curd begins to turn golden. Add the rest of the ingredients and cook until the sauce thickens. Serve hot sprinkled with freshly ground Sichuan pepper. This Chongqing dish is delicious with fried rice or noodles.

Spiced Pressed Bean Curd with Blanched Cabbage *(Xiāng Dòufu Gān Bān Xīncài)*

½ teaspoon salt
11 oz (300 g) cabbage
2 tablespoons soy sauce
½ teaspoon brown sugar

1 tablespoon sesame oil
pinch of five-spice powder
1 cup chopped spiced pressed bean
  curd

Put on a pan of water to boil. Add salt. Wash the cabbage and cut in small squares. Plunge into the boiling water for 2 minutes, then drain. Mix together the soy sauce, sugar, sesame oil and five-spice powder. Stir into the cabbage. Garnish with the chopped spiced bean curd.

This recipe is from Suzhou in Jiangsu province. In Sichuan a teaspoon of finely chopped green chilli and some shreds of Sichuan preserved vegetable (see Basic Ingredients, p. 25) would be added. Serve with boiled rice. If you like hot food include a small bowl of hot sauce.

Bean Curd with Tomatoes *(Fānqié Shāo Dòufu)*

2 cakes bean curd
2 large tomatoes
2 tablespoons cooking oil
1½ cups stock
1 tablespoon dry sherry *or* rice wine
2 teaspoons soy sauce
1 teaspoon brown sugar

1 teaspoon salt
pinch of freshly ground pepper
2 teaspoons cornflour dissolved in
  ½ cup water
1 tablespoon finely chopped green
  onion or chives

Cut the bean curd into thick strips about 1 inch (2.5 cm) long. Cut the tomatoes into quarters, then into eight pieces. Heat the oil in a wok or pan and stir-fry the tomatoes for 2 minutes. Add the bean curd, stock, sherry, soy sauce, sugar, salt and pepper and mix well. Add the cornflour mixture and cook gently until the sauce thickens. Garnish with the chopped green onion or chives and serve with boiled rice or noodles.

This recipe is from Chengdu in Sichuan province.

Bean Curd with Cucumber Slices
(Piàn Guā Dòufu)

2 green onions	1 teaspoon brown sugar
1 cucumber	½ cup stock
2 cakes bean curd	1 teaspoon cornflour dissolved in 1
3 tablespoons cooking oil	tablespoon water
2 tablespoons soy sauce	2 tablespoons cooked beetroot strips

Slice the green onion. Wash the cucumber and cut in half, then cut each half lengthwise. Slice diagonally across each quarter. Chop the bean curd into small cubes. Heat oil in a wok or frying pan and stir-fry the green onion for 1 minute. Add the cucumber and fry for another minute. Add the soy sauce, sugar, stock and bean curd. Cook together for 2 more minutes on a gentle heat. Add the cornflour mixture and turn up the heat. Cook until the sauce thickens. Garnish with the beetroot strips.

This recipe is from Shanghai.

Bean Curd with Pickles
(Chǎo Dòufu Xiǎocài)

2 cakes bean curd	½ teaspoon salt
3 tablespoons cooking oil	2 tablespoons soy sauce
2 tablespoons finely chopped	2 teaspoons brown sugar
pickled gherkins *or* cucumbers	pinch of five-spice powder
1 tablespoon finely chopped	1 tablespoon finely chopped green
pickled vegetables	onion or chives
½ teaspoon finely chopped ginger	

Squeeze the bean curd in a cloth to remove excess moisture. Crumble into small pieces. Heat the oil in a wok or pan and stir-fry for 2 minutes. Keep breaking up the curd as you fry and cook until the curd begins to turn golden. Stir in the rest of the ingredients, mix well and fry for another 2 minutes. Serve sprinkled with the green onion.

This blend of sweet and sour tastes is enjoyed in the Shanghai cuisine.

Bean Curd with Pickled Red Cabbage
(Suān Cài Shāo Dòufu)

7 oz (200 g) pickled red cabbage	½ teaspoon salt
2 cakes bean curd	pinch of five-spice powder
3 tablespoons cooking oil	pinch of freshly ground pepper
2 tablespoons soy sauce	1 tablespoon finely chopped green
1 teaspoon sugar	onion *or* chives

Drain the pickled cabbage, retaining the juice, and chop. Chop the bean curd in cubes. Heat oil in a wok or frying pan and stir-fry the cabbage for 1 minute. Add the soy sauce, sugar, salt, five-spice powder and bean curd. Stir together. Add ½ cup water to ½ cup of the pickle liquid and pour over. Allow to cook on a gentle heat for 3–4 minutes. Sprinkle with pepper. Garnish with green onion and served with boiled rice.

In Jiangsu province, other pickled or salted greens are used in this recipe. Salted vegetables should always be soaked in cold water for 30 minutes before use.

Fried Bean Curd with Vegetables
(Chǎo Dòufu Cài)

2 cakes bean curd	1 carrot
2 tablespoons soy sauce	1 cup green beans
2 tablespoons dry sherry *or* rice wine	cooking oil
1 teaspoon cornflour dissolved in 1	1 teaspoon finely chopped ginger
tablespoon water	1 cup bean sprouts
2 green onions	1 teaspoon salt
1 green pepper	pinch of freshly ground pepper
2 cups cauliflower *or* broccoli florets	2 teaspoons brown sugar
2 tomatoes	

Cut the drained bean curd into small cubes. Mix together the soy sauce, sherry and cornflour liquid. Stir the curd into this mixture and leave to stand for 15 minutes. Meanwhile, chop the green onions. Cut the green pepper in half, core and cut into small strips. Cut the cauliflower florets into small pieces. Cut the tomatoes into quarters, then into eight pieces. Peel the carrot and slice diagonally. Slice the beans diagonally into small pieces. Heat 2 tablespoons oil in a wok or frying pan and stir-fry the bean curd and its marinade until all the liquid is absorbed. Remove from the pan. Add a little more oil and stir-fry the green onion and ginger for 1 minute. Add the cut vegetables and bean sprouts and sprinkle with salt, pepper and sugar. Stir-fry for 1 minute, then add the fried bean curd. Mix together, adding a little stock if necesary. Serve hot with boiled rice.

Red-cooked Bean Curd *(Hóngshāo Dòufu)*

This recipe illustrates the technique of 'red' cooking, popular in Shanghai. It is a form of braising in which the food is cooked in a sugary sauce made of rice wine, soy sauce, ginger and fragrant stock. Its effect is to give the food a deep red-brown tinge. The cooking time must be long enough to make the sauce thick without the use of a thickening agent. Zhejiang province, to the south, supplies the rice wine for the technique, as it does the vinegar used in sweet-and-sour cooking.

4 cakes bean curd	*For the marinade*:
Chinese cabbage *or* crisp lettuce, chopped	1 teaspoon finely chopped ginger
1 tablespoon finely chopped green onion	1 teaspoon finely chopped garlic
	4 tablespoons soy sauce
	½ cup stock
	4 tablespoons dry sherry *or* rice wine
	1–2 tablespoons brown sugar
	1 teaspoon salt
	1 teaspoon five-spice powder
	2 teaspoons sesame oil

Cut the drained bean curd into small cubes. Mix the marinade together and stir in the bean curd. Allow to stand overnight or for a few hours. Heat a pan gently and cook the bean curd and marinade until the liquid has all been absorbed or evaporated. Arrange the Chinese cabbage on a dish and turn out the bean curd on to it. Garnish with green onion. Serve with boiled rice.

Sweet-and-Sour Bean Curd Sheets
(Táng Cù Huá Miàn)

4 oz (110 g) fresh bean curd sheet (see p. 52)	2 tablespoons brown sugar
cooking oil for deep-frying	½ tablespoon dry sherry *or* rice wine
1 tablespoon soy sauce	2 teaspoons cornflour dissolved in
1 tablespoon brown vinegar	½ cup water

Cut the sheet into small rectangles (if fresh sheet is unavailable, soak dried sheets in water before use). Heat oil in a wok or frying pan and fry the sheets, a few at a time, until golden. Remove and drain. In another pan, heat the sweet-and-sour ingredients and stir until the sauce thickens. Pour over the fried bean curd sheets and serve hot with boiled rice and vegetables.

This recipe is from Tianjin in Hobei province.

Sweet-and-Sour Bean Curd with Green Pepper
(Táng Suān Dòufu Qīnjiāo)

2 cakes bean curd	1–2 tablespoons flour
4 oz (110 g) bamboo shoots	oil for deep-frying
1 green pepper	3 tablespoons vinegar
2 green onions	1 tablespoon soy sauce
2 tablespoons dry sherry *or* rice wine	1 teaspoon sesame oil
1 teaspoon salt	1 tablespoon cornflour dissolved in
1 egg, beaten	½ cup water

Cut the bean curd into large cubes. Slice the bamboo shoots and cut into strips. Cut the pepper in half, core and cut each half into a few square pieces. Chop the green onion. Mix the sherry with the salt and stir in the bean curd cubes. Allow to stand for 30 minutes. Mix in the beaten egg, then roll the cubes in flour until they are all well covered. Heat oil in a pan and deep-fry the bean curd until golden. Remove and drain. In a wok or pan, stir-fry the bamboo shoots, green pepper and green onion for 2 minutes. Add the rest of the ingredients and stir until the sauce thickens. Add the fried bean curd and mix together. Serve hot with boiled rice.

Stir-fried Bean Curd Sticks *(Chǎo Fǔ Yǐ)*

a few cloud ears *or* dried black
fungus
4 oz (110 g) dried bean curd sticks
4 oz (110 g) asparagus
2 oz (50 g) bamboo shoots
3 tablespoons cooking oil
2 tablespoons soy sauce

1 teaspoon salt
1 teaspoon brown sugar
2 tablespoons dry sherry *or* rice
wine
pinch of five-spice powder
1 teaspoon cornflour dissolved in 1
tablespoon water

Soak the fungus in hot water for 30 minutes. Break the bean curd
sticks into 2-inch (5-cm) pieces and soak in warm water for 20
minutes; drain. Boil the asparagus in slightly salted water until just
tender. Drain and cut in 2-inch (5-cm) lengths. Slice the bamboo
shoots and cut in strips. Heat oil in a wok or frying pan and stir-fry
the asparagus, bamboo shoots, fungus and bean curd sticks for 1
minute. Add the rest of the ingredients and cook until the sauce
thickens. Serve hot with boiled rice.
This recipe is from Shanghai.

Bean Curd Salad *(Qīngjiāo Bān Dòufu Tiáo)*

2 cakes bean curd
oil for deep-frying
1 cup green pepper strips
1 cup cooked beetroot strips
1 tablespoon sesame oil

½ teaspoon salt
2 teaspoons brown sugar
pinch of freshly ground pepper
pinch of five-spice powder

Cut each cake into 2 pieces and deep-fry in hot oil. When golden,
drain and slice. Cut each slice in strips, then add the green pepper
and beetroot strips. Mix the rest of the ingredients in a small bowl
and pour over the bean curd and vegetables. Serve with cold noodles. Other cold vegetables such as celery or carrot could be added
to this dish.

Stir-fried Bean Curd Balls
(Chǎo Dòufu Yuán)

2 cakes bean curd
½ teaspoon salt
1 teaspoon flour
oil for deep-frying
1 small carrot, sliced diagonally
1 stick celery, sliced diagonally
1 cup sliced mushrooms

1 cup chopped spinach
2 tablespoons soy sauce
1 tablespoon dry sherry *or* rice
wine
1 teaspoon brown sugar
2 teaspoons cornflour dissolved in
1 cup stock

Mash the drained bean curd with a fork and mix in the salt and flour. Using a little more flour, form the curd into walnut-sized balls. Heat oil in a pan and deep-fry the balls until golden. Remove and drain. Heat 3 tablespoons oil in a wok or frying pan and stir-fry the vegetables for 2 minutes. Add the rest of the ingredients and stir together well. Add the bean curd balls and cook until the sauce thickens. Serve with boiled rice or noodles.

Bean curd balls go well in a sweet-and-sour recipe or with sweet-and-sour vegetables.

Bean Curd with Potatoes
(Dòufu Yuán Chǎo Shǔ)

bean curd balls (see previous recipe)
½ lb (225 g) potatoes
cooking oil
1 cup sliced onion
1 teaspoon finely chopped garlic

1 teaspoon finely chopped ginger
½ teaspoon salt
1 tablespoon soy sauce
cucumber, sliced
fresh tomato, sliced

Prepare bean curd balls as in the previous recipe. Boil the potatoes in their skins until just tender. Cut into cubes. Heat some oil in a pan and fry the potatoes until golden. Remove, drain and keep warm. Leave about 2 tablespoons oil in the pan and stir-fry the onion, garlic and ginger for 1 minute. Add the salt and soy sauce. Put in the fried bean curd balls and potato and mix well together. Serve garnished with fresh cucumber and tomato slices.

Bean Curd with Pineapple *(Dòufu Bōluó)*

2 cakes bean curd
1 large tin pineapple chunks
1 teaspoon cornflour
2 tablespoons soy sauce

2 tablespoons dry sherry *or* rice wine
cooking oil
1 green onion, chopped
1 cup bean sprouts

Cut the drained bean curd into small cubes. Drain the syrup from the pineapple and retain 1 tablespoon of it. Dissolve the cornflour in this and stir in with the soy sauce and sherry. Stir in the curd and leave to stand for 15 minutes. Heat oil in a wok or frying pan and stir-fry the bean curd and its marinade until all the liquid is absorbed. Remove and drain. Add a little more oil and stir-fry the green onion, bean sprouts and pineapple for 1 minute. Add the bean curd and cook together for 2 minutes. Serve with boiled rice.

Bean Curd with Orange Peel and Dates
(Lǎo Chénpí Dòufu Piàn)

1 orange	1 teaspoon finely chopped ginger
½ cup dates	1 teaspoon finely chopped garlic
2 cakes bean curd	1 teaspoon salt
cooking oil	2 tablespoons soy sauce
1 green onion	1 tablespoon chopped walnuts

Peel the orange and slice the peel into 1 inch (2.5 cm) strips. Squeeze out the flesh and keep the juice. Cut the dates in half and stone them. Slice the bean curd. Heat 3 tablespoons oil and stir-fry the curd until it begins to brown. Remove and keep warm. Add a little more oil if necessary and stir-fry the green onion, ginger and garlic for 1 minute. Add the orange peel and dates, salt, soy sauce and 2 tablespoons orange juice. Stir-fry together for 2 minutes and add the bean curd. Allow to warm through. Garnish with walnuts and serve hot with boiled rice.

In China, the orange peel might be replaced by tangerine peel.

The Cook's Tasty Bean Curd
(Dàshīfu De Dòufu Měiwèi)

½ lb (225 g) flat noodles	2 tablespoons soy sauce
3 tablespoons cooking oil	2 tablespoons dry sherry *or* rice wine
1 small onion, sliced	1 tablespoon sesame oil
1 cup sliced broccoli	3 cakes bean curd, cut into small
1 cup sliced fresh mushrooms	pieces
½ cup sliced water chestnuts	2 teaspoons sesame seeds
½ cup sliced bamboo shoots	2 tablespoons cashew nuts
1 cup bean sprouts	2 tablespoons chopped green
2 cloves garlic, finely chopped	onions
1 teaspoon finely chopped ginger	2 tablespoons chopped green
1 teaspoon salt	peppers
1 teaspoon brown sugar	

Heat a pan of salted water and boil the noodles until tender. Rinse, drain and keep warm on a serving dish. Heat the oil in a wok or pan and stir-fry the onion, broccoli, mushrooms, water chestnuts and bamboo shoots for 2 minutes. Add the bean sprouts and fry for a further 1 minute. Remove, put them on the dish with the noodles and keep warm. Add a little more oil and fry the garlic and ginger for 1 minute. Stir in the salt, sugar, soy sauce, sherry and sesame oil. Add the bean curd pieces and fry gently until the curd begins to brown. Mix together with the noodles and vegetables. Keep warm. Add a little more oil to the pan and fry the sesame seeds, nuts, green onion and pepper until the nuts begin to brown. Use as a garnish for the noodles and bean curd.

Bean Curd with Steamed Asparagus and Mushrooms *(Dòufu Lóngxūcài Dōng Gū)*

½ cup dried black mushrooms
2 cakes bean curd
2 tablespoons cooking oil
1 teaspoon salt
1 teaspoon finely chopped ginger
1 teaspoon finely chopped garlic
½ lb (225 g) asparagus

1 cup leeks, sliced
2 tablespoons soy sauce
2 tablespoons dry sherry *or* rice wine
½ cup stock
1 teaspoon cornflour dissolved in the mushroom water

Soak the mushrooms in a cup of boiling water for 20 minutes. Drain, retaining the water, and slice. Drain the bean curd and cut into small pieces. Heat the oil in a wok or pan and stir-fry for 3 minutes. Remove and sprinkle with the salt, ginger and garlic. Cut the asparagus into small pieces. Put the leeks in the bottom of a heatproof dish or pan. Spread half of the bean curd over this and half of the mushrooms on top of the bean curd. Put in the asparagus. Cover with the rest of the bean curd and finally the mushrooms. Mix the rest of the ingredients to make a sauce and pour over the vegetables. Put the dish in a steamer and steam on a high heat for 15 minutes or until the asparagus is tender.

Fried Bean Curd with Hearts of Green *(Chǎo Dòufu Càixīn)*

½ cup dried mushrooms
½ lb (225 g) spring greens *or* broccoli
½ lb (225 g) Chinese cabbage *or* crisp lettuce
1 cup stock
½ teaspoon salt
½ teaspoon brown sugar
4 cakes bean curd

cooking oil
2 green onions, chopped
2 teaspoons finely chopped garlic
1 teaspoon finely chopped ginger
2 tablespoons soy sauce
2 tablespoons dry sherry *or* rice wine
pinch of freshly ground pepper
1 teaspoon cornflour dissolved in 1 tablespoon water

Soak the dried mushrooms in hot water for 30 minutes. Wash the greens and cabbage and shred. Put in a pan with the stock. Add salt and sugar and simmer gently for 5 minutes. Drain the greens and cabbage but keep the liquid. Cut the bean curd into small pieces and fry in ½ cup oil until the curd begins to turn golden. Remove from the pan. Drain and slice the mushrooms. Keep the oil hot and stir-fry the mushrooms, green onion, garlic and ginger for 2 minutes. Add the soy sauce, sherry and pepper. Mix well. Add the fried bean curd and stir. In a small pan, add the cornflour mixture to the greens liquid and stir over a gentle heat until the sauce thickens. Put the bean curd and mushrooms in the centre of a serving dish. Arrange the greens and cabbage around the edge. Pour over the sauce. Serve hot with boiled rice.

Soup *(Tāng)*

In China, soup is served as a meal in itself or a thinner soup will be served between dishes to help the food go down. Like tea, a clear tasty soup can be an excellent refresher at the end of a full meal.

Vegetable Soup *(Càitāng)*

2 tablespoons cooking oil
1 onion *or* 2 green onions, sliced
3 cups chopped mixed vegetables
2 teaspoons salt
½ teaspoon freshly ground pepper

2 tablespoons soy sauce
2 pints (1 litre) water
1 bunch watercress, cleaned and
  chopped

Heat the oil in a soup pot and stir-fry the onion for 1 minute. Add the vegetables, salt, pepper and soy sauce and fry together for 2 minutes. Add the water and bring to the boil. Allow to simmer until all the vegetables are tender. Add the watercress or serve garnished with chopped fresh coriander leaf.

Bamboo Shoot and Mushroom Soup
(Sǔn Xiānmó Tāng)

1 cup sliced bamboo shoots	1 tablespoon soy sauce
2 tablespoons cooking oil	1 teaspoon salt
2 green onions	pinch of freshly ground pepper
1 teaspoon finely chopped garlic	2 pints (1 litre) stock
½ cup sliced mushrooms	

Cut the sliced bamboo shoots into small squares. Heat the oil in a soup pan and stir-fry the green onion and garlic for 1 minute. Add the bamboo shoots and mushrooms and fry for 1 minute. Add the soy sauce, salt, pepper and stock. Bring to the boil and lower the heat to simmer for 5 minutes. Serve hot with boiled rice and slices of cucumber.

Four Delicacies Soup *(Sì Bǎo Tāng)*

1 aubergine	1 teaspoon salt
2 courgettes	pinch of freshly ground pepper
2 tablespoons cooking oil	1 bunch watercress, cleaned and
2 green onions, chopped	chopped
1 teaspoon finely chopped ginger	1 egg
2 pints (1 litre) stock	1 tablespoon soy sauce
2–4 tomatoes, cut into quarters	

Wash the aubergine and courgettes. Slice the aubergine, then cut each slice into four pieces. Slice the courgettes. Heat the oil in a soup pan and stir-fry the green onion and ginger for 1 minute. Add the aubergine and courgette pieces and fry for 2 minutes. Pour in the stock. Add the tomatoes, salt and pepper and simmer until the aubergines are tender. Add the watercress and cook for 5 more minutes. Beat the egg and pour slowly over the surface of the hot soup. As the egg cooks, it becomes the characteristic 'egg flower'. Sprinkle with soy sauce and serve.

Bean Curd Balls in Vegetable Soup
(Dòufu Yuán Càitāng)

bean curd balls (see p. 62)
2 pints (1 litre) vegetable soup (see
   p. 67)

Prepare bean curd balls and vegetable soup as in the recipes. Put the balls into the soup and serve hot with fried bread or sesame rolls.

Three Delicacies Soup *(Sān Bǎo Tāng)*

2 tablespoons cooking oil
1 cup sliced asparagus
1 cup chopped spinach
1 teaspoon salt

1 teaspoon brown sugar
pinch of five-spice powder
2 pints (1 litre) stock
1 cup sliced cucumber

Heat oil in a soup pan and stir-fry the asparagus for 2 minutes. Add the spinach and fry for a further 1 minute. Sprinkle on the salt, sugar and five-spice powder and pour in the stock. Simmer until the asparagus is tender. Meanwhile, cut each cucumber slice into four pieces. Put in the soup and simmer for 3 minutes. Serve hot.

Bean Curd Soup with Mushrooms *(Dōng Gū Dòufu Tāng)*

4 dried mushrooms
1 cake bean curd
2 pieces bamboo shoot
1 carrot
1 green onion
2 tablespoons cooking oil
2 pints (1 litre) stock

2 tablespoons soy sauce
2 teaspoons dry sherry *or* rice wine
1 teaspoon sesame oil
pinch of five-spice powder
2 teaspoons chopped fresh
  coriander leaf

Soak the dried mushrooms in warm water for 20 minutes. Drain and discard the stems. Cut each top into four. Cut the curd into four, then slice each piece in half again and cut diagonally to make triangles. Slice and cut the bamboo shoots into similar shapes. Peel and slice the carrot and cut the slices into thick sticks. Chop the green onion. Heat the oil and stir-fry the green onion for 30 seconds. Add the bean curd, mushrooms, bamboo shoots and carrot and stir-fry for 2 minutes. Add the stock, soy sauce and sherry. Bring to the boil. Stir in the sesame oil and five-spice powder and serve hot, garnished with the coriander leaf.

Green Jade Soup *(Yùshì Tāng)*

The Chinese are very fond of spinach. It frequently lends dishes a deep green colour, known as 'green jade'.

1 tablespoon cooking oil
1 onion, chopped
1 teaspoon finely chopped ginger
2 tablespoons chopped bean curd
7 oz (200 g) spinach, chopped

2 pints (1 litre) stock
1 teaspoon salt
pinch of freshly ground pepper
pinch of five-spice powder

Heat the oil in a soup pan and fry the onion for 2 minutes. Add the ginger, bean curd and spinach and fry for 1 minute. Add the stock, salt, pepper and five-spice powder and bring to the boil. Stir and simmer for 10 minutes.

Green Jade Asparagus Soup
(Yùshì Lóngxūcài Tāng)

2 tablespoons cooking oil
1 teaspoon finely chopped ginger
1 teaspoon finely chopped garlic
7 oz (200 g) asparagus, cut in small
  pieces
1 stick celery, sliced diagonally
½ cup red radishes, cut in halves
1 tablespoon soy sauce

1 tablespoon sesame oil
1 teaspoon salt
pinch of freshly ground pepper
2 pints (1 litre) stock
½ lb (225 g) spinach, chopped
1 teaspoon finely chopped fresh
  mint

Heat the oil in a soup pan and stir-fry the ginger and garlic for 30 seconds. Add the asparagus, celery and radishes and fry for 1 minute. Add the soy sauce, sesame oil, salt, pepper and stock. Bring to the boil and simmer for 15 minutes. Add the spinach, stir and cook for a further 10 minutes. Serve garnished with the mint.

Pressed Bean Curd Soup *(Dòufu Gān Tāng)*

2 cakes bean curd
cooking oil
4 green onions *or* 1 onion, sliced
1 cup fresh green peas
1 cup chopped tomatoes
½ cup sweet corn

2 tablespoons soy sauce
2 tablespoons dry sherry *or* rice wine
1 teaspoon brown sugar
2 teaspoons salt
1 tablespoon sesame oil
2 pints (1 litre) stock or water

Press the bean curd as described on p. 51, and sliver. Heat 4 tablespoons cooking oil in a wok or pan and fry the curd until golden. Remove and drain. Fry the green onion for 30 seconds, add the rest of the vegetables and fry for another 1 minute. Add the remaining ingredients except the stock and mix well. Transfer to a soup pot. Put in the bean curd and stock and heat gently. Serve hot.

Mongolian Tea *(Měng Gū Chá)*

The Mongolian plains are noted for their strong dusty winds. This 'tea' is a rich warming soup designed to refresh the rider after a tiring day in the saddle.

1 green onion
2 tablespoons butter *or* clarified
  butter *or* margarine
1 cup oats

1 teaspoon salt
2 pints (1 litre) stock
2 cups goat's milk *or* cow's milk

Chop the green onion and fry in butter for 1 minute. Add the oats or other available cereal and salt and stir in the hot butter for a further minute. Pour on the stock and simmer gently until a thick gruel is produced (about 15 minutes). Pour on the milk and mix well.

The tea can be served immediately or it will keep if simmered gently. Vegetables could be added as long as a little butter, cereal and milk accompanies them. Goat's milk gives the authentic taste, but cow's milk or cream is quite acceptable in this soup. Serve hot with some flat bread.

Cassia Corn Soup *(Guì Yùmǐ Tāng)*

1 teaspoon finely chopped ginger
1 tablespoon dry sherry *or* rice
  wine
1 tablespoon soy sauce
1 egg
2 pints (1 litre) stock
1 teaspoon salt
7 oz (200 g) sweet corn

1 stick cinnamon, broken into
  pieces
1 tablespoon ground almonds
2 teaspoons cornflour dissolve in 2
  tablespoons water
1 tablespoon finely chopped green
  onion

Mix the ginger with the sherry and soy sauce. Beat the egg. Bring the stock to the boil and add the salt, sweet corn, marinated ginger, cinnamon and ground almonds. Allow to simmer for 10 minutes. Stir in the cornflour mixture and the egg. Serve hot garnished with the green onion.

This recipe is from Jiangsu province.

Egg Flower Soup *(Xiānmó Dànhuā Tāng)*

1 egg
pinch of salt
½ cup sliced mushrooms
2 tablespoons soy sauce
2 teaspoons cornflour dissolved in
  2 tablespoons water

2 pints (1 litre) stock
1 teaspoon salt
pinch of freshly ground pepper

Beat the egg, adding a pinch of salt. Soak the mushrooms in the soy sauce and cornflour mixture. Bring the stock to the boil and put in the mushrooms and the marinade. Stir in the salt and pepper.

Pour in the beaten egg as the soup boils. This creates the effect known as 'egg flower' as the egg cooks in the hot soup.

Egg Flower Soup with Spinach
(Bōcài Dànhuā Tāng)

2 pints (1 litre) stock
2 tablespoons cooking oil
1 cup chopped green onion
2 teaspoons sesame seeds
3 eggs
½ teaspoon salt

½ teaspoon freshly ground pepper
2 tablespoons soy sauce
1 tablespoon dry sherry *or* rice wine
1 cup finely chopped spinach
1 teaspoon five-spice powder

Put the stock on to boil. Heat the oil in a pan and stir-fry the green onion for 1 minute. Add the sesame seeds and stir-fry for another minute. Put into the hot stock. Beat the eggs and add the salt, pepper, soy sauce and sherry. Stir the egg mixture into the boiling stock. Stir in the spinach and lower the heat. Stir in the five-spice powder and cook gently for 3 minutes. Serve hot with hot fried bread.

Egg Flower Soup with Sweet Corn
(Dànhuā Yùmǐ Tāng)

1 egg
1 cup sweet corn
2 tablespoons soy sauce
2 tablespoons dry sherry *or* rice wine
2 teaspoons cornflour dissolved in
   2 tablespoons water

2 pints (1 litre) stock
1 teaspoon salt
pinch of freshly ground pepper
2 cloves
1 tablespoon ground almonds

Beat the egg, adding a pinch of salt. Soak the sweet corn in the soy sauce, sherry and cornflour mixture. Bring the stock to the boil and put in the sweet corn and the marinade. Stir in the salt, pepper and cloves. Pour in the beaten egg as the soup boils. Serve hot sprinkled with ground almonds.

White Radish Soup *(Lóbo Sī Tāng)*

7 oz (200 g) white radish
2 tablespoons cooking oil
1 green onion, chopped
2 tablespoons dry sherry *or* rice wine
4 tablespoons soy sauce

2 pints (1 litre) stock
2 teaspoons salt
2 teaspoons sesame oil
1 tablespoon finely grated carrot

Peel and shred the radish. Heat the oil in a soup pan and stir-fry the green onion for 30 seconds. Pour in the sherry, half of the soy sauce and stock. Add the radish and salt and simmer gently until the radish is tender. Stir in the sesame oil and the rest of the soy sauce just before serving. Serve garnished with grated carrot.

Other roots such as turnip, swede or parsnip could be substituted for the white radish. This recipe is from Hangzhou in Zhejiang province.

Marrow Soup *(Gúsuĭ Tāng)*

22 oz (600 g) marrow
1 tablespoon salted black beans
2 tablespoons cooking oil
1 onion, sliced
1 teaspoon finely chopped ginger
1 teaspoon salt
2 pints (1 litre) stock

1 tablespoon soy sauce
1 teaspoon sesame oil
pinch of five-spice powder
2-inch (5-cm) piece cucumber
1 tablespoon finely sliced green
   onion

Peel the marrow and cut into cubes. Soak the black beans for 30 minutes in a cup of warm water. Heat the oil in a soup pan and fry the onion for 2 minutes. Add the ginger and marrow cubes and fry for 1 minute. Add the salt, stock and black beans with their water and simmer until the marrow is tender. Stir in the soy sauce, sesame oil and five-spice powder. Cut the cucumber into thick slices and cut each slice into quarters. Serve the soup garnished with the cucumber and green onion. This soup is delicious with sliced pickled vegetables.

Hot and Sour Soup *(Là Suān Tāng)*

2 eggs
1 teaspoon salt
2 tablespoons soy sauce
½ teaspoon five-spice powder
1 tablespoon cornflour dissolved in
   1 cup water

2 pints (1 litre) stock
3 tablespoons vinegar
pinch of fresh ground Sichuan
   pepper

Beat the eggs. Mix together the salt, soy sauce, five-spice powder and cornflour liquid. Put the stock on to boil and stir in the salt and cornflour mixture. As the soup comes to the boil, pour in the eggs. Add the vinegar and pepper.

This is a basic soup from Sichuan. The recipe becomes more interesting and substantial if you add some Sichuan preserved vegetable, dried or fresh mushrooms and some slices of spicy pressed bean curd. More heat can be added by including chopped green chilli or ½ teaspoon chilli powder.

Chinese Cabbage and Green Onion Soup (*Báicài Cōng Tāng*)

12 oz (350 g) Chinese cabbage *or*
  crisp lettuce
2 tablespoons cooking oil
2 green onions, chopped
½ teaspoon salt

2 tablespoons soy sauce
2 pints (1 litre) stock
1 teaspoon finely grated orange
  peel

Wash the cabbage and shred. Heat the oil in a soup pan and stir-fry the green onion for 1 minute. Add the cabbage, salt, soy sauce and stock. Simmer for a few minutes. Serve garnished with the orange peel.

Mushroom Soup (*Dōng Gū Tāng*)

2 oz (50 g) dried mushrooms
2 tablespoons cooking oil
1 green onion, chopped
1 teaspoon finely chopped garlic
1 teaspoon finely chopped ginger

1 tablespoon soy sauce
1 teaspoon brown sugar
½ teaspoon salt
2 pints (1 litre) stock

Soak the mushrooms in water for 20 minutes. Separate the stems from the caps and discard the stems. Heat the oil in a soup pan and fry the green onion, garlic and ginger for 2 minutes. Add the mushrooms and fry for a further 2 minutes. Add the soy sauce, sugar and salt and mix together. Pour in the stock and simmer gently with the lid on for 30 minutes.

Pickled Vegetable Soup *(Suāncài Tāng)*

½ cup pickled beetroot
½ cup pickled cucumbers
½ cup pickled cauliflower
2 tablespoons cooking oil
2 green onions, chopped
1 teaspoon finely chopped ginger
½ lb (225 g) marrow chunks, peeled
½ cup shredded Chinese cabbage *or* lettuce *or* white cabbage

1 teaspoon salt
pinch of freshly ground pepper
juice of ½ lemon
2 pints (1 litre) stock
1 bunch watercress, cleaned and chopped
1 tablespoon chopped fresh coriander leaf

Slice the pickled vegetables. Heat the oil in a soup pan and fry the green onion and ginger for 2 minutes. Add the marrow and cabbage and fry for a further 2 minutes. Sprinkle with salt and pepper and the lemon juice. Pour in the stock and add the watercress and pickled vegetables. Simmer together for 15 minutes. Serve hot, sprinkled with coriander leaf.

This soup is excellent in cold weather, served with hot breads.

Tales of Mu:
Quiet Persistence Soup

Mu, the cook whose rare abilities have assured him a place in legend was once asked how he came to make Quiet Persistence Soup. His employer, Lord Wang, attested to the fact that it was his favourite soup. Mu's story went something like this:

It was near the end of a humid summer. Mist began to gather over the hills as evening fell and already the cherry leaves were changing colour. It was as if Lord Wang was filled with the restlessness of the day, when his old friend, Chan, called. Chan put his hand on Wang's shoulder.

'I find you with such a frown, old friend,' said Chan. 'Someone has written *yi* across your forehead!'★

Lord Wang grunted. 'Huh! There is an affair of one which I must but cannot settle. A certain official is standing in my way like a wall of rock. I have beaten my head against it to find a solution. I haven't been able to eat for days. Mu is complaining. This weather doesn't help either. The air in the city is like thick soup!'

Chan stroked his beard thoughtfully. 'Soup. Hmm . . . When the sage rules the world he takes soup – or is it water? – as his guide.'

'That old chestnut!' Lord Wang snorted. 'It will take more than water to wash away that one!'

'That may be true, my friend, but it is not good to be off your food like this. Let us pay your cook a visit.'

During the past few days, Mu had fasted along with his employer. But today he resolved to take a little soup to keep his strength up. Using a recipe recommended by a woman in the village, he had prepared a tureen of nourishing soup with which he would also endeavour to serve his master. But as he went to carry the heavy tureen, his arms shook with the weakness of the fast and the contents flew out into the garden. When the two

★The written character *yī* ('one') looks like a straight horizontal line.

noble friends arrived in the kitchen, they found Mu sitting on the doorstep. He rose awkwardly and bowed.

'So your master gives you nothing to do now,' Chan laughed.

Mu bowed again. 'Before the arrival of your honours, there was a mishap with the soup. I found myself watching it dripping across the stones outside the kitchen window. Though I did not notice it happening, suddenly I see a tiny stream has made its way as far as the street.' He gestured with his hand.

The three men watched as the trickle of soup moved across the stone pathway. Mu continued: 'When it found an obstacle in its path it sought another way. Where no way was to be found, it won through by quiet persistence.'

Lord Wang turned to his friend, his face beaming. 'That's it!' he exclaimed. He bent down and, dipping a noble finger delicately in the soup, he put it to his lips. 'That is certainly it!'

Chan stared at his friend. Mu's mouth had dropped open in bewilderment. Lord Wang laughed.

'Why . . . Quiet Persistence Soup!'

Legumes *(Dòu)*

Legumes are given a separate chapter since they contain more protein than most vegetables. In the same way, soya bean curd *(dòufu)* will be found with its own chapter.

Beans with Mushrooms
(Huì Xiānmó Wāndòu)

3 tablespoons cooking oil
2 green onions, chopped
1 teaspoon finely chopped ginger
1 teaspoon finely chopped garlic
1 cup shelled broad beans *or* other
  fresh beans
1 cup sliced fresh mushrooms

2 tablespoons soy sauce
2 tablespoons dry sherry *or* rice wine
1 teaspoon salt
1 teaspoon brown sugar
1 cup stock
1 teaspoon cornflour dissolved in 1
  tablespoon water

Heat the oil and stir-fry the green onion, ginger and garlic for 1 minute. Add the beans. Add mushrooms and fry for a further minute. Stir in the soy sauce, sherry, salt, sugar and stock and cook gently until the beans are tender. Add the cornflour mixture and cook until the sauce thickens. Serve with noodles or rice.

This recipe is from Shandong province where lima beans would take the place of the broad beans.

Sweet-and-Sour Beans
(Táng Cù Wāndòu)

1 lb (450 g) shelled broad beans *or* lima beans
2 tablespoons cooking oil
2 tablespoons finely chopped green onion

For the sauce:
1 teaspoon finely chopped garlic
1 teaspoon finely chopped ginger
pinch of freshly ground pepper
2 tablespoons vinegar
1 tablespoon brown sugar
pinch of salt
2 teaspoons cornflour dissolved in ½ cup water

Boil the beans in slightly salted water until they are just tender. Heat the oil in a wok or pan and stir-fry the beans for 3 minutes. Remove and keep warm. Put the sauce ingredients into the pan and mix over a gentle heat until the sauce thickens. Stir the beans into the sauce and garnish with the green onion. Serve with boiled rice.

Green Beans with Garlic and Ginger
(Jìdòu Suàn Jiāng Yóu)

3 tablespoons cooking oil
½ tablespoon finely chopped ginger
3 cloves garlic, finely chopped
½ lb (225 g) green beans, trimmed and sliced

1 teaspoon salt
1 teaspoon brown sugar
1 tablespoon soy sauce
1 tablespoon sesame oil
1 tablespoon dry sherry *or* rice wine

Heat the oil and fry the ginger and garlic for 30 seconds. Add the green beans and stir-fry for 1 minute. Add the rest of the ingredients and mix well. Lower the heat and cook until the beans are tender. Serve hot.

Frozen beans are excellent in this recipe. If fresh beans are used it may be necessary to add ½ cup water to ensure that they become tender. A teaspoon of chilli pepper oil may be added to give this Sichuan dish its hot flavour.

Green Beans with Fried Bean Curd
(*Jìdòu Chǎo Dòufu*)

2 cakes bean curd	½ lb (225 g) French beans
4 tablespoons cooking oil	1 teaspoon salt
2 tablespoons soy sauce	1 teaspoon cornflour dissolved in 2
1 tablespoon dry sherry *or* rice wine	tablespoons stock

Cut the drained bean curd into small cubes. Heat 2 tablespoons oil in a wok or frying pan and fry the curd until it begins to turn golden. Remove and marinate in the soy sauce and sherry. Cut the beans into pieces about 2 inches (5 cm) long. Heat 2 tablespoons oil and stir-fry the beans for 1 minute. Sprinkle with salt. Add the bean curd and marinade. Mix together and stir in the cornflour liquid. Cook gently until the sauce thickens. Serve hot with boiled rice.

Soya Beans with Black Mushrooms
(*Dōng Gū Huángdòu*)

2 cups dried soya beans	2 cloves garlic, finely chopped
salt	2 teaspoons cornflour dissolved in
1 cup dried black mushrooms	1 cup mushroom *or* bean liquid
3 tablespoons cooking oil	2 tablespoons soy sauce
1 small onion, chopped	2 tablespoons dry sherry *or* rice wine

Soak the beans in water for a few hours or overnight. Add 1 teaspoon salt and boil the beans until tender (about 1½ hours). Drain, retaining the bean water. Meanwhile soak the mushrooms in 2 cups boiling water for 30 minutes. Drain thoroughly, retaining the water. Slice the mushrooms. Heat the oil in a wok or pan and fry the onion and garlic until the garlic begins to brown. Add the mushrooms and ½ teaspoon of salt and fry for 2 minutes. Add the cornflour mixture to the fried mushroom. Stir in the cooked beans, soy sauce and sherry. Cook together until the sauce thickens.

Soya Beans with Cashew Nuts
(*Huángdòu Yǎoguǒ*)

2 cups soya beans	1 tablespoon sesame oil
1 teaspoon salt	2 tablespoons soy sauce
3 tablespoons cooking oil	½ teaspoon salt
2 tablespoons cashew nuts	1 teaspoon brown sugar
1 cup green peas	1 teaspoon cornflour dissolved in
1 cup sliced fresh mushrooms	½ cup bean water

Soak the beans overnight in water with 1 teaspoon salt added. Boil until tender, then drain (keep the bean water for the cornflour). Heat the oil in a wok or pan and fry the cashew nuts until they begin to turn golden. Remove from the pan. Add the beans, peas and mushrooms and stir-fry for 2 minutes. Add the rest of the ingredients. Mix well and put in the fried nuts. Cook on a gentle heat until the sauce thickens.

Peanuts may be substituted for the cashew nuts but the flavour of the dish will be different. Other kinds of large dried beans may be cooked in the same way.

Black Beans with Bean Curd *(Dòuji Dòufu)*

1 cup dried red beans
1 tablespoon soy sauce
1 teaspoon brown sugar
1 cup stock
2 cakes bean curd
2 tablespoons cooking oil
1 green onion, chopped

1 teaspoon finely chopped garlic
1 green chilli, seeded and finely
  sliced
1 tablespoon salted black beans
pinch of freshly ground Sichuan
  pepper *or* black pepper

Soak the dried beans in water for a few hours or overnight. Boil in slightly salted water until tender. Drain and mash. Stir the soy sauce and sugar into the stock and mix with the mashed beans. Cut the bean curd into small cubes. Heat the oil and stir-fry the green onion, garlic and green chilli for 30 seconds. Add the salted black beans, bean curd and mashed red beans. Cook over a gentle heat for 5 minutes. Sprinkle with pepper and serve.

This hot tasty recipe, which gains its flavour from the salted black beans, is from Chongqing ('repeated good luck'), the most important industrial city of south-western China, in Sichuan province.

Stir-fried Green Beans *(Jiàngkǎo Sìjìdòu)*

½ lb (225 g) green beans *or* string
  beans
2 tablespoons cooking oil
1 cup stock
1 tablespoon brown bean sauce

2 teaspoons soy sauce
1 teaspoon brown sugar
pinch of red chilli powder

Wash the beans and cut into 2-inch (5-cm) lengths. Heat the oil and stir-fry the beans for 2 minutes. Add the stock, cover and simmer for 3 minutes. Stir in the brown bean sauce, soy sauce, sugar and chilli pepper and cook on a high heat until the liquid is nearly evaporated.

Stir-fried Snow Peas *(Chǎo Biǎndòu)*

The whole flat green pod of the snow pea is cooked and eaten. They are especially prized in Beijing.

½ lb (225 g) snow peas
4 tablespoons cooking oil
1 teaspoon salt
1 tablespoon chopped green onion
1 teaspoon finely chopped garlic

1 tablespoon brown bean paste
1 tablespoon soy sauce
1 teaspoon brown sugar
1 teaspoon sesame oil

Wash the pea pods and remove any string. Heat 2 tablespoons oil and stir-fry the pods over a high heat for 1 minute. Sprinkle with salt. Add a cup of water, cover and cook for 2 minutes. Drain and keep warm. Heat another 2 tablespoons oil and stir-fry the green onion and garlic for 30 seconds. Add the snow peas, bean paste, soy sauce, sugar and sesame oil, mixing well together.

Braised Green Peas *(Báiyóu Huìwāndòu)*

½ lb (225 g) fresh or frozen green
  peas
1 tablespoon cooking oil
pinch each of salt and pepper
1 cup stock

1 tablespoon dry sherry *or* rice
  wine
½ teaspoon brown sugar
1 teaspoon cornflour dissolved in 1
  tablespoon water

Rinse and drain the peas. Heat the oil in a wok or frying pan and stir-fry the peas for 1 minute. Sprinkle on a pinch of salt and pepper. Add the stock and sherry, cover and simmer for 5 minutes. Stir in the sugar and the cornflour mixture and cook gently until the sauce has thickened. Serve hot with rice or noodles. More salt may be added, according to taste.
  This recipe is from Chengdu in Sichuan.

Beans with Chestnuts *(Dòu Lìzī)*

1 cup dried red beans
1 cup shelled chestnuts
3 tablespoons cooking oil
2 green onions, chopped
1 teaspoon salt
1 tablespoon soy sauce
1 tablespoon dry sherry *or* rice wine

1 tablespoon sesame oil
1 teaspoon cornflour dissolved in 1
  cup stock
1 teaspoon finely chopped
  coriander leaf
1 teaspoon finely chopped almonds

Soak the dried beans for a few hours or overnight in slightly salted water, then boil until tender. Boil the chestnuts until tender, then cut in halves. Heat the oil and stir-fry the green onion for 30 seconds. Add the beans and chestnuts and cover with the hot oil. Sprinkle on the salt, soy sauce, sherry, sesame oil and cornflour mixture. Cook until the sauce thickens. Garnish with the fresh coriander leaf and almonds and serve with boiled rice.

Beans with Three Delicacies *(Dòu Sān Bǎo)*

1 cup dried beans
½ cup dates
4 tablespoons cooking oil
1 teaspoon finely chopped ginger
1 teaspoon finely chopped garlic
½ cup pickled cucumber *or* other
    pickled vegetable, sliced

3 tablespoons soy sauce
3 tablespoons dry sherry *or* rice
    wine
1 teaspoon brown sugar
1 teaspoon cornflour
½ cup sliced cooked beetroot

Soak the beans for a few hours or overnight in water with a little added salt, then boil them until tender. Drain, keeping the bean water. Meanwhile, boil the dates in slightly salted water for 5 minutes. Heat oil in a pan and fry the ginger and garlic for 1 minute. Add the beans, dates and pickles and stir-fry for 3 minutes. Add the soy sauce, sherry and sugar and keep over a low heat. Dissolve the cornflour in 1 tablespoon of bean water. Stir into the beans and dates. Cook on a gentle heat until the sauce thickens, adding more bean water if required. Cut the beetroot slices into strips to garnish.

Vegetables *(Cài)*

Three Vegetables in Hot Sour Sauce
(Sān Cài Làcùjiàng)

1 cup sliced turnip
1 cup sliced mushrooms
1 cup sliced bamboo shoots
3 tablespoons cooking oil
1 teaspoon finely chopped ginger
2 tablespoons soy sauce
1 tablespoon chilli sauce

1 tablespoon vinegar
1 teaspoon brown sugar
1 teaspoon cornflour dissolved in 1 cup stock
1 tablespoon finely sliced green onion

Cut the vegetables into strips. Heat the oil in a wok or frying pan and stir-fry the ginger and vegetable strips for 2 minutes. Add the rest of the ingredients (except the green onion) and cook for 3 minutes or until the sauce thickens. Garnish with the green onion and serve with rice.

Mixed Vegetable Delicacies *(Chǎo Cài Bǎo)*

14 oz (400 g) mixed vegetables
4 tablespoons cooking oil
2 green onions, chopped
2 teaspoons salt
2 teaspoons brown sugar

2 tablespoons soy sauce
2 teaspoons cornflour dissolved in
   ½ cup stock
2 teaspoons sesame oil

Make your own choice of vegetables so that the total blend is a balance of colour, flavour and texture. Choose small amounts from bamboo shoots, bean sprouts, broccoli and cauliflower florets, carrots, mushrooms, peas, sweet corn, green beans. Slice the bamboo shoots into small rectangles; cut broccoli or cauliflower into small florets; slice carrots diagonally; slice mushrooms or leave tiny mushrooms whole; slice green beans diagonally.

Heat the oil in a wok or pan and stir-fry the green onions for 30 seconds. Add the 'hard' vegetables and fry for 1 minute. Add the 'soft' vegetables and fry for 2 minutes. Add the salt, sugar, soy sauce and cornflour mixture. Mix well. Stir in the sesame oil and cook until the sauce thickens. Serve hot with rice or noodles.

Fried Sliced Vegetables *(Chǎo Cài Piàn)*

cooking oil
9 oz (250 g) vegetables, sliced
1 green onion, sliced
1 teaspoon finely chopped ginger
1 teaspoon salt
1 tablespoon soy sauce
pinch of freshly ground pepper

1 teaspoon brown sugar
1 teaspoon red chilli powder
pinch of freshly ground Sichuan
   pepper
1 tablespoon sesame oil
1 teaspoon cornflour dissolved in 1
   cup water

Heat the oil in a wok or pan until hot and fry the vegetable slices for 2 minutes. Remove from the pan and allow to cool. Add a little more oil and fry the green onion and ginger for 1 minute. Stir in the rest of the ingredients except the cornflour mixture. Add the sliced vegetables and stir together. Add the cornflour mixture and keep cooking gently until the sauce thickens.

This dish features the blending of sour, hot, salt, sweet and aromatic elements which is characteristic of the Sichuan cuisine.

Braised Vegetables *(Dùn Shí Jĭn)*

2 small aubergines	2 cloves garlic, finely chopped
2 small green peppers	1 tablespoon dry sherry *or* rice wine
2 small potatoes	1 teaspoon salt
1 onion	1 teaspoon brown sugar
1 tomato	2 tablespoons soy sauce
3 tablespoons cooking oil	½ cup stock

Wash the vegetables. Cut the stalk off the aubergines. Core the peppers. Clean the potatoes and remove blemishes but do not peel. Trim the onion and tomato. Cut all the vegetables into small pieces. Heat the oil in a pan until hot and fry the garlic for 30 seconds. Add the vegetable pieces and fry for a few minutes to lightly brown. Add the rest of the ingredients, mix together, cover and simmer gently until the vegetables are tender. Serve hot with rice.

This recipe is from the Beijing cuisine.

Fried Vegetables Beijing Style *(Chăo Yăoguŏ Cài)*

4 tablespoons cooking oil	2 tomatoes, sliced
1 cup cashew nuts	1 tablespoon dry sherry *or* rice wine
1 onion or leek, chopped	1 teaspoon brown sugar
1 teaspoon finely chopped ginger	2 tablespoons soy sauce
1 cup bean sprouts	2 teaspoons cornflour dissolved in
½ cup chopped cucumber	½ cup water
½ cup sliced bamboo shoots	

Heat 2 tablespoons cooking oil in a wok or pan and gently fry the nuts until golden. Remove from the pan. Add 2 more tablespoons oil and fry the onion and ginger for 1 minute. Add the rest of the vegetables and stir-fry for 3 minutes. Mix in the rest of the ingredients and the fried nuts and cook together until the sauce thickens. Serve hot with rice.

Other combinations of vegetables can be used; simply keep in mind the balance of taste, texture and colour.

Four Kinds of Vegetables *(Sù Cài Sì Yàng)*

1 carrot	2 tablespoons soy sauce
1 small turnip	1 tablespoon dry sherry *or* rice
½ small cabbage	wine
2 tomatoes	1 cup stock
3 tablespoons cooking oil	1 teaspoon cornflour dissolved in 1
2 teaspoons salt	tablespoon water
2 teaspoons brown sugar	1 tablespoon finely sliced green
pinch of freshly ground pepper	onion *or* chives

Wash the vegetables. Peel and trim the carrot and turnip. Slice the carrot diagonally. Slice the turnip and cut in strips. Chop the cabbage into small rectangles (the hard core can be sliced if not too stringy). Cut the tomatoes into quarters. Heat the oil in a wok or pan and stir-fry the vegetables for 2 minutes. Add the salt, sugar, pepper and soy sauce. Stir together and add the sherry and stock. Cover and simmer for 5 minutes. Stir in the cornflour mixture and cook until the sauce begins to thicken. Garnish with the green onion. Serve hot with rice or noodles.

This recipe is from Shanghai.

Six Kinds of Vegetable Delicacies *(Liù Yàng Cài Bǎo)*

Here is another Shanghai recipe in which the sauce is the same as that of the previous recipe. This time more delicate vegetables are featured which provide contrasts in flavour and texture. The dates enhance the soft sweetness which often characterizes the Shanghai cuisine.

2 tablespoons cooking oil	1 teaspoon salt
2 tablespoons bamboo shoots, cut	1 tablespoon brown sugar
in strips	1 tablespoon soy sauce
2 tablespoons bean sprouts	2 tablespoons dry sherry *or* rice
2 tablespoons radishes, halved	wine
2 tablespoons dates, cut in half and	1 teaspoon cornflour dissolved in
stoned	½ cup stock
2 tablespoons small cucumber cubes	1 tablespoon finely sliced green
2 tablespoons carrot, cut in strips	onion *or* chives
2 tablespoons sliced fresh	
mushrooms	

Heat the oil in a wok or pan and stir-fry the vegetables for 1 minute. Add the salt, sugar, soy sauce, sherry and cornflour mixture. Cook until the sauce thickens. Garnish with the green onion. Serve hot with rice or noodles.

Vegetables 'Fishy Flavour' *(Yúxiāng Cài)*

cooking oil
½ lb (225 g) vegetables, sliced
1 green onion, sliced
1 green chilli, seeded and sliced
1 teaspoon finely chopped ginger
1 teaspoon finely chopped garlic
1 teaspoon salt

1 tablespoon soy sauce
½ teaspoon chilli powder *or* 1
    teaspoon chilli sauce
1 tablespoon vinegar
pinch of freshly ground Sichuan
    pepper
1 teaspoon sesame oil

Heat 2 tablespoons oil in a wok or pan and stir-fry the vegetable slices for 2 minutes. Remove and keep warm. Add a little more oil and fry the green onion, chilli, ginger and garlic for 1 minute. Stir in the rest of the ingredients and the fried vegetables. Mix well and cook for 3 minutes. Serve hot with rice.

This is a typical hot sauce from Sichuan. The name 'fishy flavour' refers to the combination of ginger, garlic, chilli and vinegar. The proportions may be changed according to taste.

Three Fried Delicacies *(Chǎo Sān Yàng)*

2 small onions
2 small tomatoes
1 green pepper
3 tablespoons cooking oil

1 teaspoon salt
pinch of freshly ground pepper
1 teaspoon brown sugar

Cut the onions and tomatoes into quarters. Cut the green pepper into pieces about the same size. Heat the oil in a wok or pan and stir-fry the onion for 30 seconds. Add the green peppers and fry for 1 minute. Add the tomatoes, salt, pepper and sugar and cook for a further 1 minute. Serve with a bean curd or bean dish and boiled rice.

Braised Asparagus *(Lóngxūcài Shāo)*

1 lb (450 g) asparagus
1 carrot
3 tablespoons cooking oil
1 cup stock
1 teaspoon salt

1 teaspoon brown sugar
1 tablespoon dry sherry *or* rice
    wine
1 teaspoon cornflour dissolved in 1
    cup water

Remove and discard the hard ends of the asparagus stalks. Boil the stalks in a little salted water until they begin to soften. Meanwhile peel and cut the carrot into long thin strips. Heat the oil and fry the asparagus for 2 minutes. Add the carrot and the rest of the ingredients except the cornflour mixture and bring to the boil. Lower the heat and cook gently until the asparagus is tender. Add the cornflour mixture and cook until the sauce thickens. If you use tinned or frozen asparagus, simply modify the cooking process to achieve the same result.

This Beijing-style dish may be served with marinated mushrooms and rice.

Fried Aubergine *(Zhá Qiézi Piàn)*

11 oz (300 g) aubergine	½ teaspoon salt
cooking oil for deep-frying	2 teaspoons brown sugar
1 green onion, chopped	½ cup stock
2 tablespoons soy sauce	1 teaspoon sesame oil

Wash the aubergine and cut off the stalk. Slice and cut each slice into diamond shapes. Heat the oil in a wok or deep-frying pan until hot and deep-fry the aubergine until golden. Remove and drain. In another pan, add a tablespoon of hot oil and stir-fry the green onion for 30 seconds. Add the aubergine, soy sauce, salt, sugar and stock. Cook for 2 minutes until the liquid is almost evaporated. Mix in the sesame oil and serve hot with rice.

Spicy Aubergine Slices *(Xiāng Qiézi Tiáo)*

7 oz (200 g) aubergine	1 tablespoon dry sherry *or* rice wine
cooking oil	
2 green onions, finely sliced	2 teaspoons chilli sauce
1 teaspoon finely chopped ginger	2 teaspoons cornflour dissolved in ½ cup stock
1 teaspoon finely chopped garlic	
4 oz (100g) fresh mushrooms, sliced	pinch of freshly ground Sichuan pepper
1 tablespoon soy sauce	

Wash the aubergine and cut off the stalk. Slice and cut each slice in thick strips. Heat the oil in a wok or deep-frying pan. Deep-fry the aubergine for 2 minutes. Remove and drain. In another pan, put in 1 tablespoon of hot oil and stir-fry the green onion, ginger, garlic and mushrooms for 30 seconds. Add the soy sauce, sherry, chilli sauce and fried aubergine. Mix well and cook for 2 minutes. Add the cornflour mixture and pepper and cook until the sauce thickens.

This is the Sichuan way to cook aubergine.

Fried Aubergine in Brown Bean Sauce
(Jiàng Bào Qiézi Piàn)

In this Shanghai recipe, the aubergine is presented in a sweet, but not hot, sauce.

1 lb (450 g) aubergines
oil for deep-frying
1 teaspoon finely chopped ginger
1 teaspoon finely chopped garlic
1 tablespoon finely chopped green
  onion

2 tablespoons soy sauce
2½ tablespoons sweet brown bean
  paste
½ teaspoon brown sugar
1 teaspoon cornflour dissolved in 1
  tablespoon water

Wash the aubergines and cut off the stalk. Cut lengthwise into four, cut across and finally cut these pieces into strips. Heat the oil in a wok or deep-frying pan until it is very hot. Deep-fry the strips for 30 seconds. Remove from the oil and drain. In another pan, put 2–3 tablespoons of oil. Stir-fry the ginger, garlic and green onion for 30 seconds. Add the drained aubergines and the rest of the ingredients. Cook and stir together until the sauce is thickened.

Aubergines with 'Fishy Flavour'
(Yúxiāng Qiézi)

½ lb (225 g) aubergines
cooking oil
1 green onion, sliced
1 green chilli, seeded and sliced
1 teaspoon finely chopped garlic
1 teaspoon finely chopped ginger
1 teaspoon salt
1 tablespoon soy sauce

½ teaspoon chilli powder *or* 1
  teaspoon chilli sauce
1 tablespoon vinegar
pinch of freshly ground Sichuan
  pepper
1 teaspoon sesame oil
1 tablespoon finely chopped
  walnuts *or* cashew nuts

Wash the aubergines and cut off the stalk. Cut into strips. Heat the oil in a wok or deep-frying pan and deep-fry the aubergine for 2 minutes. Remove and drain. In another pan, add 2 tablespoons of the hot oil and stir-fry the green onion, chilli, garlic and ginger for 30 seconds. Stir in the aubergine. Mix together, then add the rest of the ingredients except the sesame oil and the nuts. Cook for 3 minutes, then stir in the sesame oil. Garnish with the nuts and serve hot with rice or noodles.

Aubergines in Hot Sauce *(Là Wēi Qiézi Sī)*

11 oz (300 g) aubergines	1 teaspoon brown sugar
1 teaspoon finely chopped ginger	pinch of salt
3 tablespoons cooking oil	½ cup stock
2 tablespoons soy sauce	1 tablespoon finely chopped green
1 teaspoon chilli sauce	onion *or* chives

Wash the aubergines and cut off the stalks. Cut into thin strips and mix with the ginger. Heat the oil in a wok or pan. Stir-fry the aubergine and ginger for 2 minutes. Add the rest of the ingredients (except the green onion) and cook on a gentle heat for 3 minutes. Garnish with green onion and serve hot with rice or noodles.

Bamboo Shoots in Wine (*Sǔn Yóujìn*)

'Bamboo shoots – white like new pearls.' BO JU YI, AD 772–846.

11 oz (300 g) canned bamboo shoots	1 cup dry sherry *or* rice wine
4 tablespoons cooking oil	½ lb (225 g) Brussels sprouts *or*
1 teaspoon salt	small young greens
pinch of freshly ground pepper	1 teaspoon brown sugar
1 tablespoon soy sauce	1 cup bean sprouts

Drain the bamboo shoots and cut them in strips. Heat 2 tablespoons oil and stir-fry for 1 minute. Add the salt, pepper and soy sauce and fry for a further 2 minutes. Remove and marinate in the wine. Wash and slice the Brussels sprouts. Heat 2 more tablespoons oil and stir-fry the Brussels sprouts for 2 minutes. Add the sugar, mix well and add the bean sprouts. Fry for 1 minute. Add the marinated bamboo shoots and wine and cook together for 2 minutes. Serve hot with boiled rice.

Stir-fried Bamboo Shoots *(Chǎo Dōngsǔn)*

11 oz (300 g) canned bamboo shoots	1 teaspoon salt
2 tablespoons cooking oil	1 teaspoon brown sugar
2 teaspoons soy sauce	½ cup stock
1 tablespoon dry sherry *or* rice wine	

Drain the bamboo shoots and cut into thick slices. Heat the oil in a wok or pan and fry the bamboo shoots for 1 minute. Add the soy sauce and cook until the sauce is absorbed. Stir in the rest of the ingredients and cook gently until most of the juice is absorbed. Serve hot with a bean curd dish and rice. This recipe is from Suzhou.

Bamboo Shoots with Pickled Vegetables
(Zhá Sǔn Suāncài)

11 oz (300 g) canned bamboo shoots
cooking oil for deep-frying
4 oz (110 g) pickled vegetables, chopped
½ teaspoon salt
1 teaspoon brown sugar

½ cup stock
1 teaspoon cornflour dissolved in 1 tablespoon water
1 teaspoon sesame oil
1 tablespoon chopped fried mushrooms

Cut the bamboo shoots into small wedge-shaped pieces. Heat the oil in a wok or deep-frying pan and deep-fry the bamboo shoots for 1 minute. Remove and drain. In a separate pan, put 1 tablespoon of the oil and stir-fry the pickled vegetables for 30 seconds. Add the salt, sugar, stock and bamboo shoots and simmer over a gentle heat for 3 minutes. Add the cornflour mixture and cook until the sauce thickens. Stir in the sesame oil. Garnish with the fried mushrooms and serve hot.

Bean Sprouts with Green Pepper
(Dòuyá Qīngjiāo)

½ lb (225 g) bean sprouts
1 green pepper
3 tablespoons cooking oil
1 teaspoon salt
1 teaspoon brown sugar

2 teaspoons finely chopped garlic
1 tablespoon soy sauce
1 teaspoon chilli pepper oil (optional)

Rinse the bean sprouts and drain. Cut the pepper in half, core and remove the seeds. Cut the two halves in strips. Heat the oil in a wok or pan and stir-fry the green pepper strips for 30 seconds. Sprinkle on the salt, sugar and garlic and add the bean sprouts. Stir together for 30 seconds. Stir in the soy sauce and chilli pepper oil. Mix together and serve hot.

This dish is from Sichuan.

Stir-fried Bean Sprouts (Chǎo Dòuyá)

9 oz (250 g) bean sprouts
2 tablespoons cooking oil
1 teaspoon salt
1 teaspoon brown sugar

1 tablespoon soy sauce
1 tablespoon dry sherry *or* rice wine
1 teaspoon cornflour dissolved in ½ cup water

Rinse the bean sprouts and drain. Heat the oil in a wok or pan and stir-fry the bean sprouts for 30 seconds. Add the rest of the ingredients and fry for another minute. Serve at once and do not allow the sprouts to lose their crispness.

This recipe is from Suzhou.

Braised Broccoli *(Shāo Láncài)*

11 oz (300 g) broccoli
3 tablespoons cooking oil
1 teaspoon salt
1 teaspoon brown sugar
1 teaspoon lemon juice
½ cup stock

Wash the broccoli in a bowl of water and cut into florets. Slice the stalk. Heat the oil in a wok or frying pan and stir-fry the broccoli for 1 minute. Add the salt, sugar, lemon juice and stock. Cover and cook on a gentle heat for 3 minutes. Serve hot.

Stir-fried Cabbage *(Sū Shāo Xīncài)*

11 oz (300 g) cabbage
3 tablespoons cooking oil
4 oz (110 g) bamboo shoots, sliced
1 teaspoon salt
½ teaspoon freshly ground fennel seed
1 cup stock

Wash the cabbage, separate the leaves from the central stem and cut them into small squares. Slice the stalk thinly. Heat the oil in a wok or pan and stir-fry the cabbage and bamboo shoots for 1 minute. Add the salt, ground fennel seed and stock. Cover and simmer for 4 minutes. Serve hot with a bean curd dish and rice.

Sugar may be added to this dish for those who like sweet vegetables.

Sweet-and-Sour Cabbage *(Tián Suān Xīncài)*

11 oz (300 g) cabbage
1 green pepper
1 carrot
2 tablespoons soy sauce
2 tablespoons brown vinegar
2 tablespoons brown sugar
1 teaspoon salt
3 tablespoons cooking oil
1 green onion, chopped
½ teaspoon freshly ground pepper
1 teaspoon chilli sauce
1 teaspoon cornflour dissolved in 1 tablespoon water
2 teaspoons sesame oil

The best cabbage for this recipe is pale and crisp. Cut the cabbage into thin shreds. Cut the pepper in half, core and cut in thin strips. Cut the carrot lengthwise and cut into thin strips or 'matchsticks'. Mix together the soy sauce, vinegar, sugar and salt to make a sweet-and-sour sauce. Heat the oil in a wok or pan and stir-fry the green onion for 30 seconds. Sprinkle with pepper. Add the cabbage, green pepper and carrot and fry for 1 minute. Stir in the chilli sauce. Stir in the sweet-and-sour sauce. Add the cornflour mixture and cook until the sauce thickens. Stir in the sesame oil and serve hot with rice.

Stir-fried Cauliflower *(Chǎo Càihuā)*

1 small cauliflower
3 tablespoons cooking oil
1 teaspoon salt
1 teaspoon brown sugar
pinch of freshly ground pepper

1 tablespoon soy sauce
½ cup stock
1 teaspoon cornflour dissolved in 1 tablespoon water

Wash the cauliflower in a bowl of hot water. Cut the head into florets. Slice the tender stalk, discarding wilting leaves and stringy stalk. Heat the oil in a wok or pan and stir-fry the cauliflower for 2 minutes. Add the salt, sugar, pepper, soy sauce and stock and simmer gently until the cauliflower is nearly tender. Stir in the cornflour mixture and cook until the sauce thickens. Serve hot.

Braised Cauliflower *(Dùn Càihuā)*

11 oz (300 g) cauliflower
6 oz (150 g) carrot
3 tablespoons cooking oil
1 teaspoon salt
1 teaspoon brown sugar

pinch of freshly ground pepper
1 cup stock
1 teaspoon cornflour dissolved in 1 tablespoon water

Wash the cauliflower and cut into florets. Boil them in a little salted water until they begin to soften. Remove and drain. Meanwhile peel the carrot and slice diagonally across the root. Heat the oil in a wok or pan and stir-fry the cauliflower and carrot slices for 2 minutes. Add the salt, sugar and pepper during the frying. Add the stock or equivalent amount of cauliflower water and simmer gently until the cauliflower is tender. Add the cornflour mixture and cook until the sauce thickens. Serve hot with rice or noodles.

Stir-fried Celery *(Chǎo Qíncài)*

11 oz (300 g) celery
2 tablespoons soy sauce
1 teaspoon brown sugar
2 tablespoons cooking oil
½ teaspoon salt

pinch of freshly ground Sichuan
  pepper
1 tablespoon finely sliced green
  onion

Wash the celery. Do not discard any good green leaves; chop them. Cut the stalks lengthwise, then cut in 2-inch (5-cm) pieces. Mix with the soy sauce and sugar. Heat the oil in a wok or frying pan and stir-fry the celery for 2 minutes. Sprinkle on the salt and pepper and cook for a further minute. Garnish with the green onion. Serve hot with rice and bean curd.

Chinese Cabbage with Chestnuts *(Báicài Lìzī)*

1 cup chestnuts
2 tablespoons cooking oil
1 Chinese cabbage *or* small crisp
  cabbage, chopped
1 teaspoon salt
1 tablespoon soy sauce

1 teaspoon brown sugar
1 cup stock
pinch of five-spice powder
1 teaspoon cornflour dissolved in 1
  tablespoon water

Peel the chestnuts and boil in salted water until soft. Remove from the water and slice. Meanwhile, heat the oil and fry the cabbage for 2 minutes. Stir in the salt, soy sauce, sugar and stock and cook until the cabbage is tender. Sprinkle on the five-spice powder and stir in the cornflour mixture. As soon as the sauce thickens, pour into a serving dish and garnish with the sliced cooked chestnuts.

Lettuce may be substituted for the Chinese cabbage, but will require hardly any cooking time: fry for 30 seconds. Cashew nuts or walnuts may be substituted for the chestnuts. These should be gently fried in hot oil for 2 minutes rather than boiled.

Sweet-and-Sour Chinese Cabbage *(Tián Suān Báicài)*

The elegance of Hangzhou ('city across the river') inspired the saying: 'Above there is Heaven. Below there are Hangzhou and Suzhou.' The silk centre of China, noted for its beautiful West Lake

(Xi Hu) and bamboo groves, this is the capital of Zhejiang province. The city has been virtually rebuilt since 1949 after the large-scale destruction during periods of rebellion and war. Special Hangzhou dishes include sweet-and-sour vegetables.

11 oz (300 g) Chinese cabbage	½ teaspoon Sichuan peppercorns
½ tablespoon soy sauce	1 small green chilli, seeded and
1 tablespoon vinegar	finely sliced
½ tablespoon brown sugar	1 teaspoon cornflour dissolved in 1
2 tablespoons cooking oil	tablespoon water

Wash the cabbage and chop into rectangular pieces about 2 inches (5 cm) long. Mix the soy sauce, vinegar and sugar together. Heat the oil in a wok or pan and stir in the Sichuan peppercorns for 2 minutes. Remove and discard. Add the green chilli and cabbage and stir-fry for 2 minutes. Stir in the sweet-and-sour mixture. Add the cornflour mixture and cook until the sauce thickens.

If a crisp lettuce is substituted for the Chinese cabbage, fry for 1 minute only.

Braised Chinese Cabbage *(Áo Báicài)*

11 oz (300 g) Chinese cabbage	1 tablespoon soy sauce
2 tablespoons cooking oil	2 teaspoons salted black beans
1 green onion, chopped	2 cups stock

Wash the cabbage and chop. Heat the oil in a wok or frying pan and stir-fry the green onion for 30 seconds. Add the cabbage. Stir well and add the soy sauce, salted black beans and stock. Cover and simmer for a few minutes until the cabbage is tender. Serve hot.

Lettuce is a very satisfactory substitute in this recipe from Beijing.

Chinese Cabbage Sichuan Style *(Là Zhì Báicài)*

1 Chinese cabbage *or* large crisp	½ teaspoon salt
lettuce	1 teaspoon chilli pepper oil
2 tablespoons sesame oil	2 teaspoons brown sugar
2 teaspoons finely chopped ginger	1–2 tablespoons vinegar
1 carrot, cut into thin shreds	1 teaspoon sesame seeds, toasted
1–2 green chilli peppers, seeded	
and sliced	

Slice the cabbage. Rinse in slightly salted water and keep in a refrigerator or cool place for a few hours or overnight. Before serving, drain and arrange on a serving dish. Heat the oil gently in a wok or pan and stir-fry the ginger, carrot and chilli peppers for 1 minute. Add the rest of the ingredients and stir together over a low fire for 1 minute. Pour this sauce over the cabbage and sprinkle on the sesame seeds. Allow to cool before serving. Serve this tasty Sichuan dish with fried rice, noodles, salads or bread.

Stir-fried Courgettes *(Chǎo Xiǎodōngguā)*

1 lb (450 g) courgettes (zucchini)
3 tablespoons cooking oil
1 tablespoon chopped green onion
½ teaspoon finely chopped garlic

1 teaspoon salt
1 teaspoon brown sugar
2 tablespoons stock

Wash the courgettes and trim. Cut lengthwise, then cut across each slice diagonally to make diamond shapes. Heat the oil in a wok or frying pan and stir-fry the green onion and garlic for 30 seconds. Add the courgettes and fry for 30 seconds. Sprinkle on the salt, sugar and stock and cook together for 1 minute. Serve hot with another dish with contrasting colour and texture.

Marrow or other squashes could be substituted for the courgettes. Cut into small diamond-shaped chunks about 1 inch (2.5 cm) long. A thick-skinned marrow should be peeled before frying.

Steamed Cucumber *(Zhēng Huángguā)*

2 cucumbers
1 teaspoon salt
½ teaspoon five-spice powder

Wash the cucumbers and cut across to make 3 or 4 pieces. Slice each piece lengthwise. Cut each slice into strips. Place on a dish or in a steamer and sprinkle with salt and five-spice powder. Cover and steam until the cucumber is tender. The time may vary from 10 to 25 minutes according to taste.

Stir-fried Cucumber *(Chǎo Huángguā)*

11 oz (300 g) cucumber
7 oz (200 g) tomatoes
3 tablespoons cooking oil
½ tablespoon dry sherry *or* rice
  wine

2 tablespoons soy sauce
2 teaspoons brown sugar
½ teaspoon salt

Wash the cucumber and cut lengthwise in two. Cut across the pieces to make moon-shaped slices. Do the same with the tomatoes. Heat the oil and stir-fry the cucumber and tomato for 1 minute. Stir in the sherry. Mix in the rest of the ingredients and cook for 2 minutes.
  This recipe is from Shanghai.

Stir-fried Green Onion *(Chǎo Cōng)*

4 tablespoons cooking oil
4 green onions, chopped
1 teaspoon salt
pinch of freshly ground pepper

Heat the oil in a wok or pan and stir-fry the onions for 1 minute. Sprinkle on the salt and pepper and fry until the white part of the onion begins to turn golden. Serve as a garnish for rice or noodles. Chopped fried beancurd and nuts could be added to this garnish to give more nourishment to a plain dish.

Sesame Onions with Peanuts *(Zhīmá Cōng Huārén)*

cooking oil
½ cup peanuts
3 tablespoons sesame oil
4 green onions, chopped
1 teaspoon sesame seeds

½ teaspoon five-spice powder
1 teaspoon salt
2 teaspoons soy sauce
1 tablespoon dry sherry *or* rice
  wine

Put a thick-bottomed pan on a medium fire and put in ½ tablespoon oil. Roll the peanuts in the hot oil and gently roast them until they are well browned. Remove from the pan. Add the sesame oil and gently stir-fry the green onions for 2 minutes. Add the sesame seeds in the last 30 seconds. Add the rest of the ingredients and the peanuts and mix well for a further 2 minutes. Serve hot.

Stir-fried Green Peppers *(Chǎo Qīngjiāo)*

9 oz (250 g) green peppers
3 tablespoons cooking oil
½ teaspoon salt

½ teaspoon brown sugar
½ cup stock

Wash the peppers. Cut in half, core and cut into small squares or triangles. Heat the oil and stir-fry the peppers for 30 seconds. Add the salt, sugar and stock and cook for 2 minutes or until the peppers are tender. Serve hot with rice and bean curd.

Stir-fried Green Peppers with Salted Black Beans *(Qīngjīao Chǎo Dòuji)*

2 tablespoons salted black beans
½ cup dry wine *or* dry sherry
½ lb (225 g) green peppers
cooking oil

salt and freshly ground pepper
1 teaspoon brown sugar
1 teaspoon soy sauce

Leave the beans to soak in the dry wine. Meanwhile, wash the peppers and cut them lengthwise in two. Remove the cores and seeds and cut into thin strips. Heat 2 tablespoons of oil in a wok or pan until hot. Stir-fry the peppers until they begin to soften. Sprinkle on a pinch of salt and pepper during the cooking. Transfer to a plate. Sprinkle on the sugar and soy sauce. Tip the beans into a strainer and allow to drain. (The salty wine may be retained to be used in stock.) Heat another tablespoon of oil and stir-fry the beans for 30 seconds. Add the seasoned peppers. Stir together and serve hot.

This recipe is from Chengdu, capital of Sichuan province.

Green Peppers with Cucumber and Dates *(Chǎo Qīngjīao Guā Zǎo)*

2 green peppers
½ cucumber
½ cup dates
3 tablespoons cooking oil

½ teaspoon salt
2 teaspoons soy sauce
½ teaspoon brown sugar

Wash the vegetables and fruit and drain. Cut the peppers in half, remove the cores and seeds. Cut in rectangular pieces. Cut the cucumber piece in half and slice lengthwise. Cut the dates in half and remove the stones. Heat the oil and fry the dates for 1 minute.

Add the cucumber and peppers. Sprinkle on the salt, soy sauce and sugar and fry until most of the liquid is absorbed. Serve hot with mushrooms and nuts.

Stuffed Green Peppers *(Zhá Tián Qīngjiāo)*

9 oz (250 g) small green peppers
cooking oil for deep-drying

For the stuffing:
2 green onions, finely chopped
2 tablespoons cooked chestnuts *or* other nuts, mashed
2 tablespoons bean sprouts, coarsely chopped

2 tablespoons cooked dried beans, mashed
2 tablespoons finely chopped mushrooms
1 teaspoon salt
1 teaspoon brown sugar
2 tablespoons soy sauce
1 tablespoon cornflour

Wash the peppers and cut in halves or quarters as necessary. Discard the cores and seeds. Mix the stuffing ingredients together. Put a little of the stuffing in each piece of green pepper. Heat the oil in a wok or deep frying pan until hot. Place a piece of stuffed pepper, stuffing downwards, on a slotted spoon. Lower the slotted spoon into the hot oil and deep-fry for 2 minutes. Remove and drain. Arrange, stuffing side up, on a serving dish.
    This recipe is from Yangzhou in eastern China.

Creamed Lettuce *(Bā Nǎi Wōju)*

9 oz (250 g) crisp lettuce
3 tablespoons cooking oil
1 tablespoon chopped green onion
½ tablespoon dry sherry *or* rice wine

½ teaspoon salt
1 cup stock
1 tablespoon cornflour dissolved in ½ cup stock
2 tablespoons shredded fresh carrot

Wash the lettuce and shred across the stem. Heat the oil and stir-fry the green onion for a few seconds. Add the lettuce, sherry, salt and stock. Simmer gently for 1 minute. Stir in the cornflour mixture and cook until the sauce thickens. Garnish with the fresh carrot and serve hot.

Lettuce with Cashew Nuts *(Wōju Yǎoguǒ)*

1 large crisp lettuce	1 teaspoon brown sugar
cooking oil	1 cup stock
½ cup cashew nuts	pinch of five-spice powder
1 teaspoon salt	1 teaspoon cornflour dissolved in 1
1 tablespoon soy sauce	tablespoon water

Wash the lettuce and shred. Heat 2 tablespoons oil in a wok or frying pan and fry the nuts until they just begin to turn golden. Remove and drain. Add another tablespoon of oil if necessary and fry the lettuce for 1 minute. Stir in the salt, soy sauce, sugar and stock and cook for 30 seconds. Sprinkle on the five-spice powder and stir in the nuts and cornflour mixture. As soon as the sauce begins to thicken, serve hot with rice or noodles.

Deep-fried Marrow with Dates and Bamboo Shoots *(Zhá Gúsuǐ Zǎo Sǔn)*

The cooking of southern China is often seemingly overwhelmed by the dazzling array of the delicately sweet and subtly seasoned Cantonese cuisine, but it also includes the cuisine of Fujian province in which more dishes are fried than are steamed, and less oil and spices are used than in the Shanghai style. Here will be found deep-fried marrow, or winter-melon, with dates and bamboo shoots.

1 lb (450 g) marrow *or* squash *or* melon	cooking oil
11 oz (300 g) bamboo shoots	2 tablespoons soy sauce
½ cup dates	1 tablespoon dry sherry *or* rice wine
1 onion	1 teaspoon brown sugar
	1 teaspoon salt

Peel the marrow and cut into small chunks. Drain and slice the bamboo shoots. Cut the dates in half and remove the stones. Cut the onion in half and slice. Heat some oil in a wok or deep-frying pan and deep-fry the marrow, dates and bamboo shoots until the marrow is tender. Remove and drain. Mix the rest of the ingredients (except the onions) and pour over those that have been deep-fried. Keep on a gentle heat. Put the onion slices in a little of the oil and fry for 3 minutes. Remove and drain and use to garnish. serve hot with spicy noodles or rice.

Chinese Potato Pancakes
(Shí Jǐn Shǔ Bǐng)

11 oz (300 g) potatoes	1 teaspoon finely chopped ginger
1 tablespoon finely chopped green onion	sesame seeds
	flour
1 teaspoon finely chopped garlic	cooking oil for deep-frying
1 teaspoon soy sauce	

Boil the potatoes, then peel and mash. Mix in the green onion, garlic, soy sauce and ginger. Form the mixture into 8 balls. Flatten with the fingers and sprinkle on sesame seeds. Roll in flour until the cakes are well covered. Heat the oil in a wok or deep-frying pan until hot and deep-fry the cakes until golden. Drain and serve on a bed of lettuce, with a juicy vegetable dish or thick soup.

Stir-fried Potatoes *(Chǎo Tǔdòu Sī)*

China is one of the world's largest potato producers, and potatoes are becoming more and more popular there, with this vegetable already having found a place in Shandong country-style cooking. Here is an unusual treatment of potatoes for Westerners.

11 oz (300 g) potatoes	1 tablespoon soy sauce
3 tablespoons cooking oil	1 tablespoon vinegar
½ teaspoon Sichuan peppercorns	1 teaspoon salt
1 tablespoon chopped green onion	½ teaspoon brown sugar

Peel the potatoes and slice. Cut each slice into thin strips and soak in cold water for 15 minutes. Drain. Boil in slightly salted water for 2 minutes. Drain. Heat the oil in a wok or frying pan and add the Sichuan peppercorns. Fry until they darken in colour. Remove and discard. Put in the potatoes and green onion and stir-fry for 2 minutes. Add the rest of the ingredients. Mix well and serve hot.

Potatoes in Hot Garlic Sauce *(Gōng Bào Shǔ)*

Set on the banks of the great Songhua river, Harbin ('fish drying place'), the capital of the north-eastern province of Heilongjiang, lies in the heart of China's largest wheat- and corn-producing area, the Manchurian Plain. Because of this position on one of the most extensive plains in the world, Harbin is known as the gateway to China's 'Great Northern Waste'. The people of this area use garlic and white potatoes as basic ingredients in their cuisine. The popularity of potatoes is spreading throughout China, and some 38 million tons are grown each year.

1 lb (450 g) potatoes	1 green chilli, seeded and sliced
1 teaspoon salt	1 teaspoon chilli pepper oil
3 tablespoons cooking oil	½ teaspoon salt
4 cloves garlic, finely chopped	pinch of freshly ground pepper

Peel the potatoes and cut into small pieces. Put them in a pan, cover with water, add the salt and boil until the potatoes are almost tender. Drain. Heat the oil in a wok or pan and fry the garlic and chilli for 1 minute. Stir in the chilli pepper oil, salt and pepper. Add the potatoes and fry until the potatoes are cooked. Add a little warm water or stock if necessary.

Braised Pumpkin *(Dùn Nánguā)*

1 lb (450 g) pumpkin	1 teaspoon brown sugar
9 oz (250 g) leek	pinch of freshly ground pepper
4 tablespoons cooking oil	1 tablespoon soy sauce
1 teaspoon salt	½ cup stock or water

Peel the pumpkin and cut into cubes. Wash and trim the leek and chop diagonally across the stem. Heat the oil in a wok or pan and stir-fry the pumpkin pieces for 2 minutes. Add the leek and stir-fry for 1 minute. Add the rest of the ingredients, lower the heat and cook gently until the pumpkin is tender. Serve hot.

Any other squash such as marrow or melon, or a mixture of the same, may be used in this recipe.

Stir-fried Spinach *(Chǎo Bōcài)*

1 lb (450 g) spinach	1 teaspoon brown sugar
3 tablespoons cooking oil	2 tablespoons soy sauce
2 cloves garlic, finely chopped	1 teaspoon sesame oil
1 teaspoon salt	

Wash the spinach and chop across the stem. Heat the oil in a wok or pan and fry the garlic for 1 minute. Add the spinach and fry for 2 minutes. Add the rest of the ingredients, mix well and cook for a further 3 minutes. Serve hot with rice or noodles.

This recipe is from Fujian.

Spinach with Bamboo Shoots *(Bōcài Sǔn)*

14 oz (400 g) spinach
4 oz (110 g) canned bamboo shoots
3 tablespoons cooking oil
2 tablespoons stock

½ teaspoon salt
2 tablespoons soy sauce
1 teaspoon sesame oil

Wash the spinach and slice across the stem. Cut the bamboo shoots into thin triangular slices. Heat the oil in a wok or frying pan and stir-fry the spinach and bamboo shoots for 1 minute. Add the stock, cover and simmer for 1 minute. Add the salt, soy sauce and sesame oil and mix together. Serve hot with rice.

Creamed Tomatoes *(Nǎiyóu Fānqié)*

1 lb (450 g) tinned tomatoes
2 teaspoons cornflour
1 teaspoon soy sauce

2 teaspoons sesame oil
1 tablespoon finely chopped fresh
   coriander leaf

Drain the juice from the tomatoes and retain. Put the tomatoes in a pan and heat gently. Dissolve the cornflour in the tomato juice and stir into the tomatoes. Add the soy sauce and cook until the sauce thickens. Mix in the sesame oil. Garnish with the coriander leaf and serve hot with boiled rice.

Stir-fried Tomatoes *(Chǎo Fānqié)*

1 lb (450 g) tomatoes
cornflour
3 tablespoons cooking oil
2 tablespoons chopped green onion
1 teaspoon soy sauce

1 teaspoon brown sugar
½ teaspoon salt
1 teaspoon chilli pepper oil
   (optional)

Wash the tomatoes and cut in fours. Roll each piece in cornflour. Heat the oil in a wok or pan until very hot. Add the green onions and stir-fry for 30 seconds. Add the tomatoes and the rest of the ingredients. Stir and turn the tomatoes for 1 minute. Serve hot.

Stewed Turnips with Celery
(Shāo Lóbo Tiáo Qíncài)

½ lb (225 g) turnips
2 stalks celery
½ lb (225 g) cabbage *or* broccoli
1 onion
3 tablespoons cooking oil
1 clove garlic, sliced

1 teaspoon salt
pinch of freshly ground pepper
2 teaspoons brown sugar
2 tablespoons soy sauce
1 cup stock

Wash the turnip and slice. Cut each slice in strips. Slice the celery diagonally. Wash, drain and shred the cabbage. Peel and slice the onion. Heat the oil in a pan and stir-fry the onion and garlic for 2 minutes. Add the turnip strips and fry for a further 2 minutes. Add the celery and cabbage. Sprinkle on the salt, pepper, sugar and soy sauce. Mix together. Pour on the stock, cover and simmer gently until the turnip is tender (5–10 minutes). Serve with noodles or boiled rice.

Stir-fried Walnuts with Cucumber Sauce
(Chǎo Xiāngtaó Huánggua Yóu)

cooking oil
1 cup walnuts
1 tablespoon chopped green onion
½ cup chopped cucumber
½ teaspoon salt
½ teaspoon brown sugar

1 tablespoon soy sauce
1 tablespoon dry sherry *or* rice wine
1 cup stock
1 teaspoon cornflour dissolved in 1
    tablespoon water
1 teaspoon sesame oil

Heat 3 tablespoons oil in a wok or frying pan and stir-fry the nuts for 2 minutes. Remove from the pan and drain. Add another table-spoon oil and stir-fry the green onion for a few seconds. Add the cucumber and fry for 1 minute. Add the salt, sugar, soy sauce, sherry and stock and cook for a further minute. Put in the nuts. Stir in the cornflour mixture and cook until the sauce thickens. Stir in the sesame oil. Serve hot with a bean or bean curd dish and some slices of fresh cucumber and tomato.

Braised White Radish *(Gān Shāo Càidòu)*

This Hangzhou recipe for the large white radish would be suitable for the same weight of small red radishes (cut in halves), parsnip or turnip.

1 tablespoon salted black beans (see Basic Ingredients, p. 26)
14 oz (400 g) white radish
3 tablespoons cooking oil
1 tablespoon chopped green onion
1 teaspoon finely chopped ginger
1 green chilli, seeded and sliced
1 tablespoon dry sherry *or* rice wine
3 tablespoons soy sauce
1 teaspoon brown sugar
pinch of five-spice powder
½ cup stock

Wash the salted beans in a colander or sieve and drain. Peel and cut the radish lengthwise into long strips. Cut each strip diagonally into 2-inch (5-cm) pieces. Heat the oil in a wok or frying pan and stir-fry the green onion, ginger and chilli for 30 seconds. Add the black beans and radish and fry for a further 30 seconds. Add the rest of the ingredients. Stir together. Cover and simmer until the radish is tender. Serve hot.

Cold Dishes *(Bàn)*

Cucumber Strips with Chilli
(Là Huánggguā Tiáo)

1 cucumber
1 teaspoon chilli sauce
1 tablespoon soy sauce
2 tablespoons dry sherry *or* rice wine

1 tablespoon sesame oil
pinch of salt
1 teaspoon sesame seeds, toasted

Slice the cucumber lengthwise. Cut into strips. Mix the rest of the ingredients (except the sesame seeds) and pour over the cucumber. Garnish with the sesame seeds.

Sweet-and-Sour Cucumber
(*Táng Cù Bàn Huángguā*)

2 small cucumbers
1 teaspoon finely chopped ginger
1 teaspoon sesame oil
2 tablespoons vinegar

1 teaspoon soy sauce
1 tablespoon brown sugar
pinch of ground Sichuan pepper

Wash the cucumbers and cut each in four along the length. Cut into chunks 2 inches (5 cm) long. Mix with the ginger and sesame oil. Stir together the vinegar and soy sauce thoroughly with the sugar and pour over the cucumber. Sprinkle with Sichuan pepper.

Carrots with Hot Sauce *(Bàn Húlóbó Sī)*

11 oz (300 g) carrots
2 tablespoons chopped fresh
   coriander leaf
2 tablespoons finely sliced green
   onion *or* chives

For the sauce:
1 tablespoon vinegar
1 teaspoon chilli sauce *or* chilli
   pepper oil
2 teaspoons sesame oil
1 tablespoon brown sugar
1 teaspoon salt

Peel and top the carrots and shred into slivers about 2 inches (5 cm) long. Mix the sauce ingredients and pour over the carrot. Sprinkle on the green herbs and stir together.

Celery with Green Pepper and Sesame Sauce
(*Bàn Qíncài Máyóu*)

2 sticks celery
1 green pepper
1 slice ginger
1 teaspoon sesame seeds, toasted

For the sauce:
2 tablespoons soy sauce
1 tablespoon sesame oil
1 teaspoon salt
1 teaspoon brown sugar

Wash the celery and slice diagonally across the stem. Keep back the leaves. Cut the pepper in half, core and seed. Cut each half again, then slice the four quarters. Peel the ginger slice and cut into slivers. Put on a pan of slightly salted water to boil. Put the celery and green pepper in the boiling water and blanch for 30 seconds. Remove and drain. Mix the sauce ingredients together and pour this over the celery and green pepper. Chop up some of the green celery leaves and sprinkle a tablespoonful over the dish. Complete the garnish with the sesame seeds and ginger slivers. A tablespoon of vinegar or lemon juice may be added if a sour taste is preferred.

The recipe is from Suzhou.

Aubergine with Sesame Sauce
(Bàn Qiézi Piàn)

11 oz (300 g) aubergines
1 teaspoon finely chopped garlic
1 teaspoon finely chopped green
  onion
1 teaspoon chopped fresh coriander
  leaf

For the sauce:
2 tablespoons sesame paste (tahini)
½ teaspoon salt
1 teaspoon sesame oil
1 tablespoon soy sauce
1 tablespoon vinegar
1 teaspoon brown sugar

Wash the aubergines and cut off the stalks. Cut each in half lengthwise, then cut these pieces in two. Steam the aubergines until tender. Remove and cool. Mix the sauce ingredients together so that the sesame paste is well blended. Now mix in the garlic, green onion and coriander leaf. If necessary, add a little water to make the sauce. Pour over the aubergine slices.

Red and Green Salad *(Bàn Shí Jǐn)*

½ cucumber
1 carrot
½ cup red radishes
1 green pepper
¼ red cabbage
½ cup green beans

For the dressings:
soy sauce
vinegar
sesame oil

chilli pepper oil
2 tablespoons chopped green onion
  or chives
brown sugar
salt
1 teaspoon finely chopped ginger
1 teaspoon finely chopped garlic
rice wine *or* dry sherry
freshly ground pepper

Wash the vegetables and cut into pleasing shapes. Cut the cucumber diagonally and then shred, or cut lengthwise and then into thin strips. Cut the carrot diagonally and then shred into long thin strips. Slice the radishes, green pepper and beans. Chop and shred the red cabbage. Arrange altogether, or in separate batches of red and green, or in complementary dishes of red and green together. Keep cool.

Now make up the dressings according to taste. It is worth experimenting here to find the combinations you like best. Here are three suggestions:

1. Mix 3 tablespoons soy sauce, 3 tablespoons vinegar, 1 tablespoon sesame oil and 1 teaspoon chilli pepper oil.
2. Mix 2 tablespoons chopped green onion, 2 tablespoons soy sauce, 1 teaspoon sugar, 1 teaspoon salt, 2 tablespoons vinegar and 1 tablespoon dry sherry or rice wine.
3. Mix 1 teaspoon chopped ginger, 1 teaspoon chopped garlic, 1 tablespoon vinegar, 1 tablespoon dry sherry or rice wine, 1 teaspoon chilli pepper oil, 2 teaspoons soy sauce and a pinch of pepper.

Pour the dressings over the arrangements of red and green vegetables.

Spinach with Ginger Sauce
(*Jiāng Zhī Bócài*)

9 oz (250 g) spinach, chopped
4 tablespoons sesame oil
1 tablespoon finely chopped ginger

½ teaspoon salt
½ teaspoon lemon juice
½ teaspoon brown sugar

Blanch the spinach in a pan of slightly salted boiling water for 2 minutes. Drain and cool. Mix together the ginger sauce and pour over the spinach.

In Sichuan this recipe is made hotter by sprinkling over 1–2 teaspoons shredded green chilli and a pinch of chilli powder or ground dried red chilli.

Bean Sprouts with Fried Spicy Bean Curd
(*Dòuyá Chǎo Xiāng Dòufu Gān*)

11 oz (300 g) bean sprouts
2 tablespoons cooking oil
a few slices spiced pressed bean
  curd

2 tablespoons soy sauce
½ tablespoon vinegar
1 tablespoon sesame oil
½ teaspoon finely chopped ginger

Wash the bean sprouts and blanch in slightly salted boiling water for 1 minute. Remove and drain. Heat the oil in a wok or frying pan and stir-fry the bean curd until it becomes golden. Remove, drain and sliver. Mix the sauce ingredients together. Stir the bean sprouts and bean curd slivers together and pour over the sauce. Mix well and leave to stand.

Sour Vegetables *(Suān Cài)*

2 carrots
½ turnip
½ cucumber
1 tablespoon salt

3 tablespoons water
2 teaspoons brown sugar dissolved
   in 3 tablespoons vinegar
pinch of five-spice powder

Wash the vegetables and cut in thin slices lengthwise. Now fan-cut each slice. This is done by making a series of parallel cuts only ¾ of the length of each slice. Put the slices on a dish and sprinkle with the salt dissolved in water. Leave to stand in a cool place for 30 minutes. Rinse well with fresh water, drain and arrange on serving dishes. Mix the sauce ingredients and sprinkle over the vegetable slices. Allow to stand before serving.

To make Sour Vegetables in the western Chinese style, add a tablespoon of chilli sauce to the sauce and garnish with shredded green chilli.

Hot Pickled Vegetables *(Là Suān Cài Bàn)*

7 oz (200 g) pickled vegetables
1 tablespoon chilli sauce
2 tablespoons sesame oil
1 teaspoon shredded green chilli

Drain the vegetables and mix with the chilli sauce and sesame oil. Sprinkle with green chilli.

If Chinese pickles are not available, pickled cucumbers or beetroot can be used in this recipe.

Bean Curd Salad *(Dòufu Cài Bàn)*

This salad is best prepared the day before use.

4 cakes bean curd

For the marinade:
2 tablespoons dry sherry *or* rice
    wine
2 tablespoons water
2 tablespoons soy sauce
2 tablespoons vinegar
2 tablespoons sesame oil *or* soya oil
½ teaspoon salt
pinch of freshly ground pepper
pinch of ground aniseed *or* fennel
    seed *or* star anise *or* five-spice
    powder
2 teaspoons brown sugar
1 clove garlic, finely chopped

For the salad:
1 carrot, peeled and cut into small
    'matchsticks'
1 stalk celery, sliced diagonally
1 cup finely chopped cabbage
a few fresh mushrooms, sliced
2 green onions, sliced across the
    stem
½ cup fresh peanuts

Cut the bean curd cakes into small chunks. Stir the marinade ingredients together until well blended and pour over the bean curd. Keep in a cool place for some hours or overnight. Prepare the salad the following day. Dry roast the peanuts without salt until they begin to brown. Mix together all the salad ingredients. Carefully stir the marinated bean curd into this. Sprinkle with extra salt and pepper if necessary. Serve with cold spicy noodles, following with a hot dessert such as Toffee Bananas.

Fungi *(Gū)*

Fungi are widely used in China in both fresh and dried forms. Fresh mushrooms can always be used in place of dried ones, but the taste and texture will not be the same. All dried fungi should be soaked in water for 20–30 minutes before use in order to soften them. The soaking water can be retained for the stockpot.

Dried black or brown mushrooms (*dōng gū*) are one of the basic ingredients of Chinese cookery. Their name – 'winter mushroom' – refers to the time of their harvest. The *huā gū* – 'flower-like mushroom' – has a thicker cap with deep cracks on the surface. This mushroom has a distinct fragrance which gives it its other name of *xiāng gū* – 'fragrant mushroom'.

Cloud Ears or Wood Ears (*mù ěr*) is a fungus which grows on dead tree bark. It has little flavour but is added to dishes for its crunchy texture.

Any edible fungi may be used in Chinese cookery, and if you are able to identify them, you could use any wild varieties you are able to find. Some of the best fungi seem to occur in beech woods.

Experiment will soon teach you which species go best in certain dishes, and some more readily lend themselves to being dried and kept for later use. Of particular value are members of the species *Agaricus* and *Boletus*; other useful species include *Hygrophorus*, *Tricholoma* and *Russula*. The two fungi to be found in the West on dead wood are *Craterellus cornucopioides* (Horn of Plenty) and *Auricularia auricula* (Jew's Ear) which can easily be dried and used in the same way as Cloud Ears. The one essential, however, is the ability to recognize the mushroom or fungus when you see it, in order to avoid any that might be poisonous.

Mushrooms with Bean Curd
(Mógū Dùn Dòufu)

1 tablespoon cooking oil
4 oz (110 g) button mushrooms
2 cakes bean curd
½ lb (225 g) canned bamboo shoots
1 cup stock
1 teaspoon salt
1 tablespoon dry sherry *or* rice wine

2 teaspoons cornflour dissolved in ½ cup stock
1 tablespoon soy sauce
1 teaspoon sesame oil
1 tablespoon finely sliced green onion *or* chives

Heat oil in a wok or frying pan and stir-fry the mushrooms for 30 seconds. Remove and drain. Cut the bean curd into small cubes and leave to drain. Slice the bamboo shoots into thin squares. Bring the stock to the boil in a pan. Add the bean curd, bamboo shoots, salt, sherry and mushrooms. Cover and simmer for 10 minutes. Stir in the cornflour mixture and soy sauce and cook until the sauce thickens. Stir in the sesame oil. Arrange in a serving bowl and garnish with the green onion. Serve hot with rice.

Although this recipe is from Hangzhou, it could be served Northern style with hot bread.

Mushrooms with Vegetable Shoots
(Xiānmó Jiāobái)

4 oz (110 g) cauliflower *or* broccoli florets
4 oz (110 g) bean sprouts
7 oz (200 g) mushrooms
3 tablespoons cooking oil
1 green onion, chopped
1 teaspoon salt

pinch of freshly ground pepper
1 tablespoon soy sauce
1 tablespoon dry sherry *or* rice wine
½ cup stock
1 teaspoon cornflour dissolved in 1 tablespoon water

Wash the vegetables. Cut the florets into small pieces and slice the mushrooms. Heat the oil and stir-fry the green onion for 30 seconds. Add the vegetables and stir-fry for 1 minute. Sprinkle on the salt and pepper, and add the soy sauce, sherry and stock. Stir in the cornflour mixture and cook until the sauce thickens. Serve hot with rice.

This recipe is from Shandong province.

Mushrooms with Fresh Vegetables *(Xiānmó Shícài)*

1 cup green peas	1 teaspoon salt
2 tomatoes	1 teaspoon brown sugar
4 oz (110 g) green beans	1 tablespoon soy sauce
7 oz (200 g) mushrooms	1 teaspoon chilli sauce
3 tablespoons cooking oil	1 teaspoon cornflour dissolved in
1 teaspoon finely chopped ginger	½ cup stock
1 teaspoon finely chopped garlic	

Wash the peas and drain. Slice the tomatoes, beans and mushrooms. Heat the oil and stir-fry the vegetables for 2 minutes. Add the ginger, garlic, salt, sugar, soy sauce and chilli sauce. Stir together. Stir in the cornflour mixture and cook until the sauce thickens. Serve hot with rice or noodles.

This recipe is from Sichuan.

Marinated Mushrooms *(Yóujìn Xiānmó)*

Marinated vegetables are popular in Beijing cuisine. Use either fresh or dried mushrooms. The wine or spirit used for the marinade leaves room for your own experimentation.

½ lb (225 g) fresh mushrooms	*For the marinade:*
2 tablespoons cooking oil	4 tablespoons dry sherry *or* wine *or*
1 green onion, chopped	rice wine
1 teaspoon sesame seeds, toasted	1 tablespoon soy sauce
	1 teaspoon brown sugar
	pinch of salt

Wash the mushrooms and divide the caps from the stalks. Stir the marinade ingredients together and leave the mushrooms to soak in this for a few hours or overnight. Remove and drain. Heat the oil in a wok or frying pan and stir-fry the green onion for 30 seconds.

Add the mushrooms and fry for 1 minute. Sprinkle with the sesame seeds and serve hot with a bean curd dish and rice.

Fresh Mushrooms with Vegetable Sauce (*Xiānmó Yóucài*)

4 oz (110 g) green pepper
4 oz (110 g) celery
4 oz (110 g) cucumber
3 tablespoons cooking oil
1 teaspoon salt
pinch of freshly ground pepper
2 tablespoons soy sauce
1 teaspoon finely chopped ginger
1 teaspoon finely chopped garlic
1 cup stock
7 oz (200 g) sliced mushrooms
1 teaspoon cornflour dissolved in 1 tablespoon water
1 tablespoon finely sliced green onion

Wash the vegetables. Core and seed the green pepper. Cut the celery diagonally in thin slices. Cut the cucumber to make small cubes. Cut the green pepper into thin slices. Heat the oil and stir-fry the vegetables for 1 minute. Add the salt, pepper, soy sauce, ginger and garlic. Fry for another minute. Add the stock and mushrooms and cook together for 2 minutes. Stir in the cornflour mixture and cook until the sauce thickens. Garnish with the green onion and serve hot with rice or noodles.

This Beijing recipe could also be served with a Chinese bread.

Fried Mushrooms with Bamboo Shoots Beijing Style (*Chǎo Xiānggū Sǔn Piàn*)

6 dried mushrooms
9 oz (250 g) canned bamboo shoots
3 tablespoons cooking oil
2 green onions, chopped
½ teaspoon salt
1 tablespoon dry sherry *or* rice wine
1 tablespoon soy sauce
2 tablespoons stock
2 teaspoons cornflour dissolved in 2 tablespoons water
1 tablespoon slivered carrot
2 teaspoons finely chopped nuts

Soak the mushrooms in warm water for 30 minutes. Drain, discard the stalks, and slice the caps. Cut the bamboo shoots into thick slices. Heat the oil in a wok or frying pan and stir-fry the green onion for 30 seconds. Add the mushrooms and bamboo shoots and stir-fry for 1 minute. Add the salt, sherry, soy sauce and stock and cook for a further minute. Stir in the cornflour mixture and cook until the sauce thickens. Garnish with the carrots and nuts and serve hot with rice or noodles.

Fresh Mushrooms with Bamboo Shoots (*Xiānmó Sǔn*)

½ lb (225 g) fresh mushrooms
½ lb (225 g) tinned bamboo shoots
4 tablespoons cooking oil
1 teaspoon salt
pinch of freshly ground pepper
1 tablespoon dry sherry *or* rice wine

1 teaspoon brown sugar
½ cup stock
1 teaspoon cornflour dissolved in 1 tablespoon water
1 teaspoon slivered green chilli

Wash the mushrooms and drain the bamboo shoots. Slice both. Heat the oil in a wok or pan and stir-fry for 2 minutes, adding the salt and pepper during the frying. Add the sherry, sugar and stock and mix well. Stir in the cornflour mixture and cook until the sauce thickens. Garnish with the slivered chilli and serve hot with rice or noodles.

Hot Mushrooms with Bamboo Shoots (*Xiānmó Là Sǔn*)

½ lb (225 g) fresh mushrooms
½ lb (225 g) canned bamboo shoots
2 tablespoons cooking oil
½ cup chopped green onion *or* onion
1 teaspoon salt

pinch of freshly ground pepper
1 teaspoon finely chopped garlic
1 teaspoon finely chopped ginger
2 teaspoons chilli pepper oil
1 teaspoon cornflour dissolved in ½ cup stock

Wash the mushrooms and drain the bamboo shoots. Slice both. Heat the oil in a wok or pan and stir-fry the green onion for 1 minute. Add the salt, pepper, garlic and ginger and fry for 1 minute. Add the mushrooms and bamboo shoots and stir well together. Stir in the chilli pepper oil. Add the cornflour mixture and cook until the sauce thickens.

This recipe is from Sichuan.

Stir-fried Dried Mushrooms (*Chǎo Xiānggū*)

2 oz (50 g) dried mushrooms
2 tablespoons cooking oil
½ teaspoon salt
½ teaspoon brown sugar

pinch of freshly ground pepper
2 teaspoons soy sauce
1 tablespoon sesame oil

Soak the mushrooms in water for 30 minutes. Remove and drain. Discard the stalks. Heat the oil in a wok or pan and stir-fry the mushrooms for 2 minutes, sprinkling on the salt, sugar and pepper during the frying. Add the soy sauce and sesame oil and fry until the liquid is absorbed. Serve hot.

This recipe is from Guangzhou.

Dried Mushrooms in Vegetable Sauce (*Xiānggū Càiyóu*)

2 oz (50 g) dried mushrooms
3 tablespoons cooking oil
1 green onion, chopped
½ teaspoon salt
pinch of freshly ground pepper

1 tablespoon soy sauce
1 tablespoon dry sherry *or* rice wine
1 teaspoon brown sugar
1 teaspoon cornflour dissolved in 1 cup stock

Soak the mushrooms in water for 30 minutes. Drain and slice in half. Heat the oil in a wok or pan and stir-fry the green onion for 1 minute. Add the mushrooms, salt and pepper and stir-fry for 2 minutes. Add the rest of the ingredients and cook until the sauce thickens.

Deep-fried Mushrooms (*Zhá Xiānmó*)

½ lb (225 g) fresh mushrooms
salt
pepper
white of 1 egg

2 tablespoons flour
1 tablespoon water
oil for deep frying

Wash the mushrooms and separate the caps from the stalks. Sprinkle with salt and pepper. Make a batter by beating the egg white with the flour until stiff, gradually adding the water. Coat the mushrooms with the batter and deep-fry in hot oil. Drain and serve hot.

Mushrooms with Cabbage (*Chǎo Xiānmó Xīncài*)

1 small pale green cabbage
1 cup small fresh mushrooms
4 tablespoons cooking oil
1 green onion, chopped
1 teaspoon finely chopped garlic

1 teaspoon finely chopped ginger
1 teaspoon soy sauce
1 teaspoon brown sugar
½ teaspoon salt

Wash the cabbage and trim, slice and shred it. If the mushrooms are small enough, leave as they are, otherwise slice. Heat the oil in a wok or pan and stir-fry the green onion, garlic and ginger for 1 minute. Add the cabbage and the mushrooms. Stir-fry for 2 minutes until the vegetables are well covered with oil. Add the rest of the ingredients. Mix well and serve hot.

Dried Black Mushrooms with Cauliflower (*Dōnggū Càihuā*)

6 dried black mushrooms
½ lb (225 g) cauliflower
3 tablespoons cooking oil
1 green onion, chopped
1 teaspoon salt
pinch of freshly ground pepper

1 tablespoon soy sauce
1 teaspoon finely chopped garlic
pinch of five-spice powder
1 cup stock
1 teaspoon cornflour dissolved in 1 tablespoon water

Soak the mushrooms in warm water for 30 minutes. Drain, discard the stalks and slice the caps. Wash the cauliflower in a bowl of water and cut into small pieces. Slice the tender part of the stalk. Heat the oil and stir-fry the green onion for 30 seconds. Add the cauliflower and mushrooms and fry for 2 minutes. Add the salt, pepper, soy sauce, garlic, five-spice powder and stock. Simmer gently for a few minutes until the cauliflower is tender. Stir in the cornflour mixture and cook until the sauce thickens. Serve hot with rice or Chinese bread.

This recipe is from Shandong province.

Mushrooms with Carrots (*Xiānmó Húlóbo*)

1 cup fresh mushrooms
1 large carrot
3 tablespoons cooking oil
1 teaspoon salt
pinch of freshly ground pepper

1 tablespoon soy sauce
1 tablespoon dry sherry *or* rice wine
1 teaspoon cornflour dissolved in ½ cup stock

Wash the mushrooms and slice. Peel the carrot and slice diagonally across the root. Heat the oil in a wok or pan and fry the carrot for 2 minutes. Add the mushrooms, sprinkle with salt and pepper and fry for 1 minute. Add the rest of the ingredients and cook until the sauce thickens.

Mushrooms in Yellow Bean Sauce
(Xiānmó Miànjiàng)

3 tablespoons cooking oil
11 oz (300 g) button mushrooms
2 tablespoons yellow bean sauce
  (see Basic Ingredients, p. 24)
2 teaspoons cornflour dissolved in
  ½ cup stock

1 teaspoon sesame oil
1 tablespoon finely chopped fresh
  coriander leaf

Heat the oil in a wok or frying pan and stir-fry the mushrooms for
1 minute. Add the yellow bean sauce and cook for a further minute.
Add the cornflour mixture and cook until the sauce thickens. Stir in
the sesame oil. Garnish with coriander leaf and serve hot with a
bean dish and rice.

Mushrooms with Chinese Cabbage
(Dōnggū Chǎo Báicài)

6 dried mushrooms
11 oz (300 g) Chinese cabbage
3 tablespoons cooking oil
1 green onion, chopped
1 teaspoon salt

1 teaspoon brown sugar
pinch of five-spice powder
1 tablespoon soy sauce
1 teaspoon sesame oil
a few chopped walnuts

Soak the mushrooms in warm water for 30 minutes. Drain, discard
the stalks and slice the caps. Wash the cabbage and chop. Heat the
oil in a wok or frying pan and stir-fry the green onion for 30
seconds. Add the cabbage and mushrooms and fry for 2 minutes.
Add the salt, sugar, five-spice powder and soy sauce. Stir together
for 1 minute. Stir in the sesame oil. Garnish with the walnuts. Serve
hot with rice or noodles.

A crisp lettuce would be a quite suitable substitute for the cabbage
in this recipe. Fry the lettuce for 1 minute only.

Mushrooms with Cashew Nuts
(Xiānmó Yǎoguǒ)

3 tablespoons cooking oil
½ cup cashew nuts
7 oz (200 g) fresh mushrooms, sliced
1 teaspoon salt
pinch of freshly ground pepper
2 tablespoons soy sauce

1 tablespoon dry sherry *or* rice
  wine
½ cup stock
1 teaspoon cornflour dissolved in 1
  tablespoon water
1 tablespoon finely sliced green
  onion

Heat the oil and stir-fry the nuts for 2 minutes. Remove and drain. Put in the mushrooms and fry for 1 minute. Add the salt, pepper, soy sauce, sherry and stock. Stir together and mix in the fried nuts. Stir in the cornflour mixture and cook until the sauce thickens. Garnish with the green onion. Serve hot with rice or noodles.

Fresh Mushrooms with Lima Beans
(Huì Xiānmó Wāndòu)

1 cup lima beans *or* broad beans
3 tablespoons cooking oil
1 green onion, chopped
7 oz (200 g) fresh mushrooms, sliced
1 teaspoon salt
pinch of freshly ground pepper
1 teaspoon finely chopped ginger
1 teaspoon finely chopped garlic
1 tablespoon soy sauce
½ cup stock
1 teaspoon cornflour dissolved in 1 tablespoon water
1 teaspoon sesame oil

Boil the beans in slightly salted water until tender. Heat the oil in a wok or frying pan and stir-fry the green onion for 30 seconds. Add the mushrooms, sprinkle on the salt and pepper and add the beans. Stir-fry for 1 minute. Add the ginger, garlic, soy sauce and stock. Stir in the cornflour mixture and cook until the sauce thickens. Stir in the sesame oil and serve hot with rice or noodles.

This recipe is from Shandong province.

Eggs *(Dàn)*

No fowl was ever kept in the Imperial Palace. For centuries, the crowing of a cock could not be heard within the walls of the Heavenly City. Instead, as dawn broke, watchmen from Runan, specially employed for the purpose, woke the court by singing a song about the early morning.

Chickens have always been part of the Chinese country home or smallholding, however, and eggs are a part of the vegetarian diet, usually in their stir-fried or omelette form. The egg of the chicken, the most common type, is known as *jīdàn*. The duck's egg, also very popular, is *yādàn*.

Stir-fried Eggs *(Chǎo Dàn Sī)*

2 eggs
½ teaspoon salt

pinch of five-spice powder
pinch of freshly ground pepper
4 tablespoons cooking oil

Beat the eggs with the salt, five-spice powder and pepper. Heat the oil in a wok or frying pan and pour in the eggs. Stir-fry until they are well cooked and beginning to turn golden. Break up the egg as you stir-fry.

Serve on its own or mix in with rice or soup. Green onions or sliced green peppers go very well with this dish. Stir-fry a chopped onion or pepper first, then add the eggs and continue in the same way.

Sliced Omelette *(Shāo Dàn Piàn)*

2 eggs
½ teaspoon salt
pinch of five-spice powder

pinch of freshly ground pepper
2 tablespoons cooking oil

Beat the eggs with the salt, five-spice powder and pepper. Heat the oil in a frying pan until hot. Pour in the egg. Let it fill the whole pan. Lower the heat a little and let the omelette cook through. As the top begins to dry, fold the omelette in half with a slice and remove. Cut in thin slices and mix with rice, noodles or fried vegetable such as bean sprouts and mushrooms.

Green Onion Omelette *(Cōng Tān Jīdàn)*

3 eggs
pinch of salt
pinch of freshly ground pepper

pinch of five-spice powder
2 tablespoons chopped green onion
2 tablespoons cooking oil

Beat the eggs in a bowl. Mix in the salt, pepper, five-spice powder and green onion. Heat the oil in a wok or frying pan and pour in the egg mixture. Allow the egg to spread evenly. Cook for 1 minute, turn and cook the other side.

This is a basic Beijing-style omelette. Other finely chopped vegetables may be added or substituted, such as sliced mushrooms or bean sprouts.

Stir-fried Vegetables with Omelette
(Chǎo Cài Tān Dàn)

1 carrot
1 green pepper
1 stick celery
½ cup bean sprouts
2 eggs

cooking oil
1 teaspoon salt
1 tablespoon soy sauce
pinch of freshly ground pepper

Wash the vegetables and cut the carrot and green pepper into strips. Cut the celery into thin slices. Beat the eggs in a bowl. Heat 3 tablespoons of oil in a wok or pan and stir-fry the sliced vegetables for 2 minutes. Sprinkle on the salt, soy sauce, pepper and bean sprouts and fry until the carrot is tender. Transfer to a serving dish. Add a tablespoon of oil to the pan and pour in the beaten egg when the oil is hot. Let the egg spread evenly and fry on both sides until golden. Tip the omelette on top of the vegetables and serve hot.

Egg with Spinach *(Bōcài Chǎo Dàn)*

cooking oil
1 cup chopped spinach
1 teaspoon salt

1 teaspoon brown sugar
2 eggs, beaten
pinch of five-spice powder

Heat 3 tablespoons oil and stir-fry the spinach for 3–4 minutes. Add the salt and sugar. Beat the eggs into the spinach. Sprinkle with five-spice powder and stir together. Add a little more oil if necessary.

Egg with Bean Curd and Vegetables
(Dòufu Cài Chǎo Dàn)

2 cakes pressed bean curd
cooking oil
½ cup cauliflower florets, sliced
½ cup fresh mushrooms, sliced
½ cup cucumber slices
1 teaspoon salt

2 eggs, beaten
1 tablespoon dry sherry *or* rice wine
1 tablespoon soy sauce
1 teaspoon sesame oil
1 teaspoon cornflour dissolved in
    ½ cup stock

Cut the bean curd into slivers. Heat 2 tablespoons oil in a wok or pan and stir-fry until the slivers are golden. Remove from the pan. Add another 2 tablespoons oil and stir-fry the cauliflower until it begins to brown. Add the mushrooms and cucumber. Sprinkle with salt and fry together for 2 minutes. Remove from the pan. Add more oil if necessary and stir-fry the eggs until they begin to brown. Add the cooked bean curd and vegetables. Stir together and add the rest of the ingredients. Cook until the sauce thickens.

Egg with Tomatoes
(Xiān Fānqié Chǎo Dàn)

½ lb (225 g) tomatoes
3 eggs
1 teaspoon soy sauce
1 teaspoon dry sherry *or* rice wine
pinch of salt

pinch of freshly ground pepper
2 tablespoons cooking oil
1 tablespoon stock
1 teaspoon finely sliced green
onion

Cut the tomatoes into quarters, then cut each quarter again. Beat the eggs and stir in the soy sauce, sherry, salt and pepper. Heat the oil in a wok or frying pan and stir-fry the tomatoes for 1 minute. Add the beaten eggs and stir-fry until the egg thickens. Add the stock and stir together for a further minute. Garnish with the green onion. Arrange on a bed of lettuce or sliced cucumber.

Egg with Bamboo Shoots *(Sǔn Chǎo Dàn)*

In the previous recipe the eggs were cooked Suzhou-style. Here is a recipe for Shanghai-style eggs. Again, the vegetable ingredients can be varied according to taste and availability.

3 eggs
pinch of salt
pinch of freshly ground pepper
1 teaspoon dry sherry *or* rice wine
4 oz (110 g) canned bamboo shoots
cooking oil

1 teaspoon soy sauce
pinch of brown sugar
1 teaspoon sesame oil
1 teaspoon finely sliced green
onion *or* chives

Beat the eggs and mix in the salt, pepper and sherry. Cut the bamboo shoots into 'matchsticks'. Heat 1 tablespoon oil in a wok or frying pan and stir-fry the bamboo shoots for 30 seconds. Sprinkle with soy sauce and sugar and fry for a further 30 seconds. Remove from the pan. Heat another tablespoon oil and pour in the egg mixture. Add the bamboo shoots and stir together until the egg thickens. Stir in the sesame oil. Serve garnished with the green onion.

Eggs with Brown Sauce *(Hóngshāo Dàn)*

4 eggs, hard-boiled and shelled

For the sauce:
2 cups stock
½ cup soy sauce
½ cup rice wine *or* dry sherry

2 tablespoons brown sugar
1 star anise
2 cloves
½ teaspoon finely chopped ginger
½ teaspoon finely chopped garlic

While the eggs are boiling, mix the ingredients for the sauce in a pan and bring to the boil. Stir and cook for a few minutes to blend. The sauce may be used hot over the hot hard-boiled eggs or both may be allowed to cool. Keep in a cool place until needed.

If the eggs are chopped and mixed into the sauce, they make a nourishing addition to plain or fried rice. This recipe is from Jiangsu province.

Sauces *(Yóu)*

Sauces and dips have always been popular in China. Use them as marinades for vegetables before cooking or you can dunk them in sauce after cooking. The sauces are equally good with uncooked vegetables, and are delicious when spread on Chinese flat bread to eat with sliced vegetables or sliced omelette.

Sesame Soy Sauce *(Má Yóu Jiàngyóu)*

4 tablespoons soy sauce
2 tablespoons sesame oil
1 teaspoon sesame seeds, toasted
pinch of five-spice powder

Stir the ingredients together and leave to stand.

Ginger Sauce *(Shēng Jiāng Zhī)*

4 tablespoons sesame oil
1 tablespoon finely chopped ginger
1 tablespoon finely chopped green
    onion *or* chives
½ teaspoon salt

Heat the oil in a wok or pan until quite hot. Add the ginger, green onion and salt. Stir and remove from the heat. Pour into a bowl and leave to stand.

Green Onion Sauce *(Cōng Yóu)*

3 green onions, finely chopped
2 teaspoons red pepper oil (see
    Spices, p. 20)
2 teaspoons sesame oil
2 tablespoons vinegar
2 teaspoons brown sugar

1 teaspoon salt
½ teaspoon ground Sichuan
    pepper
½ teaspoon ground black pepper
2 teaspoons soy sauce
4 tablespoons cooking oil

Mix all the ingredients except the oils in a pan. Mix the oils and heat gently; then pour slowly over the mixture. Stir and leave to stand. The hot oil extracts the flavours of the ingredients.

Peanut and Sesame Sauce *(Huārén Má Yóu)* .

2 tablespoons sesame paste (tahini)
1 teaspoon finely chopped ginger
2 teaspoons brown sugar
1 tablespoon sesame oil
1 tablespoon peanut butter

½ teaspoon chilli pepper oil (see
    Spices, p. 20)
2 tablespoons soy sauce
1 tablespoon vinegar
½ teaspoon ground black pepper

Stir the ingredients together with a wooden spoon. When well mixed, add a little water if necessary to make the sauce.

Sesame seeds and whole peanuts may be used. Stir them gently in a hot pan until they are well roasted. Cool and crush them with a little oil before adding to the rest of the ingredients. Add a little water to make a sauce.

This sauce is excellent with cold noodles. For a true Sichuan flavour, garnish with blanched or stir-fried bean spouts and a teaspoon of finely chopped green chilli.

Fragrant Soy Sauce *(Xiāng Jiàngyóu)*

1 cup soy sauce
½ cup brown sugar
½ teaspoon five-spice powder

Stir the ingredients together in a pan and put on a gentle heat. Allow to bubble and keep cooking gently until the soy sauce is reduced to nearly half its volume.

Whole spices can be used in this recipe, including a small piece of cinnamon, a few seeds of fennel, cardamom or star anise. They should be removed before using the sauce as a dip.

Ginger Soy Sauce *(Jiāng Jiàngyóu)*

2 tablespoons soy sauce
2 tablespoons water
1 tablespoon dry sherry *or* rice
  wine
1 tablespoon finely chopped ginger
1 tablespoon finely chopped green
  onion

1 clove garlic, finely chopped
2 teaspoons sesame oil
1 teaspoon brown sugar
1 teaspoon brown vinegar

Stir the ingredients together and leave to stand.

Garlic Sauce *(Suàn Má Yóu)*

4 tablespoons sesame oil
1 tablespoon finely chopped garlic
  steeped in 2 teaspoons vinegar

½ teaspoon salt
1 teaspoon sesame seeds

Heat the oil in a wok or pan until quite hot. Add the rest of the ingredients, stir and remove from the heat. Pour into a bowl and leave to stand.

Chilli Sauce *(Làyóu)*

2 dry red chillis
4 tablespoons sesame oil
pinch of brown sugar

pinch of salt
½ teaspoon vinegar

Grind the chillis with a few drops of sesame oil. Continue grinding and add the sugar, salt and vinegar. Stir the mixture together with the rest of the oil to make a hot sauce.

Sesame Sauce *(Máyóu)*

2 tablespoons sesame paste (tahini)
8 tablespoons water
lemon juice

Stir the sesame paste and the water until they are well blended. Add a few drops of lemon juice to taste. This simple but nutritious sauce is delicious with brown rice.

Bean Paste Sauce *(Dòu Bàn Jiàng Yóu)*

2 tablespoons oil
2 tablespoons bean paste (yellow
  or brown)
1 teaspoon brown sugar
1 tablespoon soy sauce

Heat the oil gently in a pan and stir in the rest of the ingredients. Remove from the heat and allow to cool.

Sweet Things *(Tían Shí)*

China's largest and most populated city and the centre of its trade and industry is Shanghai ('up from the sea'). Situated on the Huangpu River, it lies only a few miles upstream from the mighty Chang Jiang (Yangtze River) which links Shanghai with the East China Sea and so the Pacific Ocean. The people of Shanghai have sweet tooths and there are sixty factories in the city producing cakes and sweetmeats *(tángguǒ)*.

Moon Cakes *(Yuè Bǐng)*

One of the great beauties of the night sky, the moon has always held a special place in China. A legend about the poet Qu Yuan (third century BC) relates that he drowned in a pool while trying to hold the moon.

   The most beautiful aspect of the moon is thought to occur around the middle of August, a phenomenon similar to the harvest moon in the West. People set out in the evening to view the moon, read and write poetry and eat moon cakes. And, of course, they will have plenty of yellow chrysanthemums.

Ideally, these cakes should be made with a Chinese moon cake mould which imprints the correct chrysanthemum-shaped pattern and Chinese characters on the cakes. The depth of the mould also aids in the filling. However, you can just as easily shape these little pies yourself. They should be about 3 inches (7 cm) in diameter. You can draw your own pattern on the cakes before baking.

4 cups flour
4 tablespoons brown sugar
½ teaspoon salt
4 oz (110 g) margarine
1 egg
1 teaspoon sesame oil

For the filling:
2 tablespoons peanuts
2 tablespoons sesame seeds
2 tablespoons walnuts *or* pine nuts

2 tablespoons chestnuts, boiled
  until tender *or* blanched almonds
2 tablespoons sultanas *or* other
  dried fruit, chopped
2 tablespoons chopped dried
  apricots
4 tablespoons brown sugar
2 tablespoons margarine
2 tablespoons rice flour *or* poppy
  seeds

Sift the flour, sugar and salt together. Cut the margarine into pieces and rub into the flour until it forms crumbs. Add enough hot water (about ½ cup) to make a pastry dough. Cover with a cloth. Roast the peanuts in a hot pan for 2 minutes. Add the sesame seeds, putting on a lid because the seeds will jump. Roast for another 2 minutes. Put the peanuts and seeds in a grinder or mortar and grind with the other nuts. Add to the rest of the filling ingredients and mix together. Roll out the pastry on a floured board. Cut rounds with a pastry cutter to fill the mould – if you have one – or make little pie cases. Rub the mould with margarine and spread pastry over the bottom and sides of the mould. Put in a tablespoon of filling. Press down gently. Wet the edges of the pastry and cover with another round to make a lid. Seal together, then remove from the mould. Put all the cakes on a greased baking tin. Beat the egg and sesame oil together and brush each cake with this mixture. This will give the tops a nice golden glaze. Bake in a hot oven (400°F/ 200°C/Gas 6) until the cakes are golden brown (about 30 minutes). Makes 16.

Steamed Sweet Buns *(Táng Bāozǐ)*

yeast dough (see Steamed
  Vegetable Buns, p. 49)

For the filling:
2 tablespoons blanched almonds *or*
  pine nuts
2 tablespoons walnuts
2 tablespoons sesame seeds

2 tablespoons peanuts, crushed *or*
  peanut butter
2 tablespoons honey
2 tablespoons brown sugar
2 tablespoons margarine *or* sesame
  oil

Grind the almonds and walnuts together with the sesame seeds. Mix with the rest of the ingredients. Put a tablespoon of the filling in the centre of a round of yeast pastry and make into buns in the same way. Steam as before.

For birthdays, these steamed buns are made to look like peaches by colouring them with yellow and red food colouring. Small pieces of pastry are shaped to make leaves and coloured green. Then they are known as *shòutáo* ('longevity peaches') and are associated with happiness and long life.

Any of your own fillings can be used. Other favourites in China are buns filled with sweet red bean paste, crystallized fruit or nuts.

Sesame Biscuits *(Zhīmá Bǐng)*

1 cup flour
pinch of salt
1 tablespoon sesame oil

1 egg, beaten
sesame seeds

Sift the flour with salt and rub in the oil to form crumbs. Mix in the egg to form a pastry dough, adding a little warm water if necessary. Roll out on a floured board and cut out biscuit-size rounds. Put the rounds on greased baking tins and sprinkle with sesame seeds. Press down the seeds gently. Bake in a fairly hot oven (400°F/200°C/Gas 6) until golden (about 15 minutes).

Sweet Potato Balls *(Zhá Fānshǔ Yuánzi)*

1 lb (450 g) sweet potatoes
3 tablespoons brown sugar
2 tablespoons flour

pinch of salt
pinch of ground nutmeg
cooking oil for deep-frying

Peel the sweet potatoes, chop and boil them in a little slightly salted water until tender. Mash. Mix with the sugar, flour, salt and nutmeg. Squeeze together to form walnut-sized balls (add a little beaten egg if necessary). Heat the oil until it is hot and deep-fry the balls until they begin to brown. Remove and drain.

Sweet Bean Paste *(Táng Dòu Jiàng)*

1 cup dried beans
honey

Soak the beans overnight in water. Boil in slightly salted water until tender. Drain. Retain the liquid. Mash the beans. Stir in enough honey to make a thick sweet paste. Add a little bean water if necessary.

Use the paste to spread on breads or stir into plain boiled rice or noodles to make a nourishing dessert.

Stuffed Dried Fruit *(Tián Gān Guŏ)*

1 cup dried whole prunes *or*
  apricots
nuts for stuffing
1 teaspoon cardamom powder *or*
  five-spice powder

If the fruit cannot be easily opened, soak for a little while in warm water. Cut open carefully and stone. Now fill each piece of fruit with whole blanched almonds or chopped nuts. Sprinkle with a small pinch of spice powder and press back together. Arrange the fruit on a serving dish with some leaves or flower heads.

Certain crystallized fruits also lend themselves well to this treatment.

Sugared Walnuts *(Táng Xiāngtáo)*

1½ cups sugar
½ cup honey
½ cup water

pinch of salt
1 tablespoon sesame oil
2 cups walnuts

Cook the sugar, honey, water and salt together for 30 minutes. When a thick syrup is made, remove from the heat and stir in the oil. Dip the walnuts in the syrup and put on a greased dish. Store in a tin or jar in a cool place.

Fresh Fruits *(Shuǐ Guǒ)*

The place of fresh fruit should not be despised when presenting a Chinese meal as it can often be a fitting and refreshing dessert. Fruit can also be very pleasant to eat between dishes instead of a more savoury soup.

A few simple measures will ensure the successful use of fruit in a meal. The fruit should always be as fresh as possible, and should be washed. Each individual fruit should be carefully chosen to harmonize with the other dish or dishes in colour, texture and taste. It should form part of the meal and not be an afterthought. These points will also affect the presentation of the fruit – what sort and colour of plate it should be served on, whether it should be served whole or cut in a certain way. Perhaps flowers, leaves or vegetables such as cucumber could be included in the presentation.

In this way, fresh fruit will often feature on the menu in China. It is particularly prized in Sichuan where it forms a pleasing contrast to hot spicy food.

Fruit in Rice Wine
(Niào Zāo Bǎi Zǐ Guǒ Gēng)

In the Feng Ze Yuan ('garden of abundance and colour') Restaurant of Beijing, the finest Shandong-style cuisine may be sampled. Marinated fruit is a speciality dessert. Although the taste and aroma of the rice wine in this recipe is primarily used to complement those of the many meat and fish dishes on the menu, fruit in rice wine can be included with vegetable dishes as long as care is taken to harmonize the dessert with the rest of the meal.

Cut the fruit so that it can easily absorb the wine. Arrange in bowls. Pour over 1 or more tablespoons of rice wine or dry sherry. Garnish with flower petals and serve at once.

In this dish, the wine is used as a sauce or syrup, and the fruit does not marinate for hours. Here is a chance for the adventurous cook to experiment with different fruits and wines. Bear in mind that the longer it marinates, the more will the taste of the fruit be changed by the wine. Spices may also be used to give special flavour and aroma to the combinations of fruit and wine you devise.

Iced Fresh Peach Slices
(Bīng Zhī Liáng Táo Fǔ)

4–6 peaches
2 tablespoons cooking oil
8 tablespoons sugar
2 tablespoons water

Skin the peaches. Cut open and remove the stones. Cut in slices. Heat the oil over a gentle heat and stir in the sugar. Stir in the water to make a thick syrup. Cover the peach slices with the syrup. Allow to cool, then chill.

This dessert goes well with bamboo shoot and mushroom soup from Sichuan (see p. 69).

Pineapples in Wine *(Bōluó Láozāo)*

1 pineapple *or* tin of pineapple
   pieces
2 cups dry sherry *or* wine
cashew nuts *or* almonds, chopped

Cut the pineapple into pieces. Strain and keep the syrup if tinned pineapple is used. Marinate the pieces in the wine overnight in a cool place. Pour over any syrup and serve chilled, garnished with the chopped nuts and a suitable flower head.

Taste a piece of the pineapple to make sure that it will blend with the rest of the meal you are preparing. This recipe is from Shandong province.

Sweet Noodles and Rice
(Mián Tián Fàn)

plain boiled noodles
plain boiled rice
sliced dry, fresh *or* crystallized fruit
syrup (optional)

Prepare enough plain noodles and rice as in the recipes. Arrange the noodles on a serving dish. Stir in half of the fruit slices and pour on a little syrup. Do the same with the rice. The two dishes may now be served separately as a dessert or the fruit rice can be carefully spooned on top of the noodles and served as one dish.

Eight Treasure Rice *(Bābǎo Fàn)*

Traditionally served at New Year celebrations and other festive occasions, this rice must contain eight treasures or charms to banish evil spirits throughout the coming year. When the eight treasures are considered to represent the eight lotus petals of Buddhism, the recipe will probably include lotus seeds. In this case, the dish is known as *Bā Bǎo Liánzi* ('lotus seed') *Fàn*. The treasures may include sweet beans, dates, almonds, peanuts, melon seeds, raisins, dried apricots, walnuts, crystallized fruits.

2 cups rice *or* glutinous rice
2 tablespoons margarine
3 tablespoons brown sugar
any available dried fruits and nuts

Wash the rice and boil until tender. Drain and stir in the margarine and sugar. Grease the bottom and sides of a pudding basin and arrange alternate layers of cooked rice with fruit and nuts. Press the fruit and nuts so that the colours will show when the dish is turned out to serve after steaming. Press the top gently and cover with foil or pieces of kitchen paper and muslin. Steam the pudding for 40 minutes. Turn out on to a serving dish and decorate with crystallized cherries, nuts and angelica.

If you have a talent for decoration, arrange a pattern of fruit at the bottom of the bowl which will show when the pudding is turned upside down on the serving dish. Layers of sweet bean paste or ground nuts could also be included with the rice to provide extra nourishment. The process can be speeded up by stirring the sweet rice, fruit and nuts together before putting in the pudding basin.

Fruit Rice *(Guǒ Fàn)*

There are many varieties of this Shandong dessert. Two are:

1. Cook 2 cups rice with water and 2 cups dried fruit, such as prunes, apricots or pears.
2. Mix cooked rice with chopped fresh or dried fruits.

In each case decorate with nuts and chopped crystallized fruit.

Toffee Apples *(Básī Píngguǒ)*

4 large eating apples	cooking oil for deep-frying
flour	4 tablespoons sugar
1 tablespoon cornflour	2 tablespoons water
2 egg whites	pinch of salt

Peel the apples and core them. Cut in quarters, then cut each quarter in half. Roll the apple pieces in a little flour. Mix 2 tablespoons flour with the cornflour and beat into the egg whites to make a batter. Heat the oil in a wok or deep-frying pan. Dip the apple pieces in the batter and deep-fry until golden. Remove and drain. Make a thick syrup by stirring the sugar and water together with the salt in a pan over a gentle heat. Stir in a tablespoon of oil. Put each apple piece in the toffee. Dip in a bowl of cold water to harden the toffee before eating. The water should be on the dining table and the toffee apples should be brought hot to the table.

This recipe is from Shandong province. Use it for other fruits such as pear, banana, small pieces of cooked yam or sweet potato. In the north, the Muslim community enjoy seeds such as lotus and melon seeds covered in toffee.

Almond Bean Curd *(Xìngrén Dòufu)*

Not a true bean curd, although the final result has the texture and appearance of bean curd.

2 cups almonds	1 tablespoon agar *or* non-animal
4 tablespoons ground rice	gelatine
1 tablespoon brown sugar	
pinch of salt	

Put the almonds in boiling water to blanch for a moment. Remove and skin. Allow to dry, then grind very finely. Stir well with the ground rice. Put in a pan and pour on 5 cups water. Stir well and leave to stand for 1 hour. Bring the mixture to the boil, lower the heat and simmer gently for 30 minutes. Strain the mixture through a straining cloth and add the sugar, salt and agar. Bring to the boil and pour into a small dish or tray to cool. Chill.

In China the curd is cut into small pieces and served with cold sweetened water. To make a more nourishing dish, substitute 2–4 tablespoons soya beans for the ground rice and grind them with the almonds. Proceed in the same way to make real almond bean curd.

This recipe is from Shanxi province.

Almond Bean Curd with Fruits
(Xìngrén Dòufu Sān Guǒ)

almond bean curd (see previous
  recipe)
fruits chosen from the
  following list:
strawberries
lichees
grapes
small pieces of peach *or* plum
small pieces of tangerine *or* orange

Cut the curd into diamond shapes and put in a serving dish. Garnish with the fruits and pour syrup over the top. This may have come from canned fruit or you can make your own syrup by dissolving a tablespoon of sugar in a cup of warm water. Allow the syrup to cool.

To make this sweet dish even more nourishing, sprinkle on finely sliced blanched almonds or finely chopped walnuts. This way of presenting almond bean curd comes from Shandong province.

Almond Bean Curd with Pineapple
(Xìngrén Dòufu Bōluó)

Make up the almond curd (see p. 138). Cut pineapple into shreds. Once the almond mixture has begun to cool, stir in the pineapple shreds and allow them to set in the curd. Garnish with nuts or segments of tangerine.

This method of allowing pineapple to set in the curd could also be used with fresh or dried fruits.

Three Iced Fruits with Nuts
(Bīng Zhēnxiū Sān Guó)

3 kinds of crystallized fruits *or* 3
  kinds of tinned fruits in syrup
1 tablespoon cooking oil
1 tablespoon walnuts, chopped

1 tablespoon cashew nuts, chopped
1 tablespoon blanched almonds,
  sliced
2–3 tablespoons caster sugar

Leave the fruit overnight in the freezing compartment of a refrigerator or in a very cool place. Cut the fruit into pieces. Heat the oil and stir-fry the nuts for 1 minute. Lower the heat. Add the sugar and roll the nuts in the sugar until they are well covered. Mix with the fruit pieces and serve.

Stir-fried 'Three Mashed Things' (Chǎo Sān Ní)

1 cup walnuts
1 cup cashew nuts
1 cup chestnuts, cooked
2 teaspoons brown sugar

3 tablespoons cooking oil
½ cup grapes, cut in halves and
  seeded *or* crystallised fruits

Mash the nuts separately, then mix together. Stir in the sugar. Heat the oil in a wok or pan and gently fry the nut mixture for a few minutes. Serve decorated with the grapes or crystallized fruits.

Fried Bananas (Chǎo Xiāngjiāo)

6 ripe bananas
3 tablespoons cooking oil *or*
  margarine
3–6 tablespoons sweet bean paste
  (see p. 134)
toasted sesame seeds

Peel the bananas. Heat the oil in a pan and fry the bananas very gently. They will become soft and the sweet juice will become like toffee in the hot oil. Just before serving spread each banana with bean paste and roll in the hot oil. Serve sprinkled with sesame seeds.

Sweet Rice Dumplings (Yuánzī)

Sweet rice dumplings were once thrown into the Mi Lo River at the time of the Dragonboat Festival (late spring) to commemorate the suicide of a poet who threw himself into the river as a protest against government policy.

2 cups glutinous rice
½ teaspoon powdered fennel *or*
  star anise *or* cardamom
large dried bamboo leaves
dates

Wash the rice and leave to soak overnight. Drain and stir in the powdered spices. Put on a pot of water to boil. Take a bamboo leaf in both hands, horizontally. Fold each end over the other to make a cone shape. You can now hold the cone quite easily in one hand, with the thumb in front of the two leaf ends and the fingers behind.

Fill each cone with about ½ cup rice and push in 2 dates. Fold up the leaf to make a little packet and tie tightly with thin string or raffia. Put the little packets in the boiling water and allow to boil until the rice is well cooked. Remove from the water and leave to cool. The packets are brought to the table to be unwrapped. Slice the dumplings and serve with sugar or honey.

If bamboo leaves are not available, aluminium foil could be used as a substitute but the packet must not be tied too tightly since the rice will expand during the cooking.

Taishan Fruit Salad *(Tàishān Sì Guǒ)*

Ancient Chinese cosmologists theorized that the earth was square, and so was China, bounded by four cardinal mountains. Emperors would make tours to the four peaks to keep an eye on the realm. Taishan ('exalted mountain'), the most easterly of the cardinal peaks, commanded the most attention since it was believed that the sun began its journey westward from there. Today, people still make the difficult climb to the summit in the hope of catching a spectacular sunrise. This is very much a matter of luck since the altitude of 5069 feet (1545 metres) above sea level ensures that the peak is frequently shrouded in mist, but if the pilgrim is blessed, he will be guaranteed a wonderful view of the countryside of Shandong province.

chopped ice
1–2 tablespoons finely chopped fresh mint
4 cups fresh *or* tinned fruit, cut in pieces
2 tablespoons icing sugar
2 tablespoons finely chopped nuts

Arrange the ice chips in a mound on a serving dish. Sprinkle with the fresh mint. Carefully arrange the fruit pieces around the four corners of the 'mountain'. Cover with mists of sugar and crushed nuts.

Fruits which lend themselves to this dish are lichees, strawberries, tangerines, peaches, pineapple and grapes. Subtle tastes and aromas may be added by a pinch of powdered spice here and there. Another version of this dessert from Shandong, and one which will commend itself to children, is to make the 'mountain' out of ice cream instead of ice chips. Then you can really go to town and make little trees and bushes out of crystallized fruit. Perhaps the odd hut or monastery, traveller or animal could feature somewhere on the slopes.

Sweet Soft Rice *(Táng Zhōu)*

1 cup glutinous rice
6 cups water
1 tablespoon brown sugar *or* honey

Wash and soak the rice. Drain. Simmer gently in the water for about 1 hour until a thick gruel is produced. Stir in the sweetening just before serving.

It is common in China to serve sweet rice gruel with small red beans. Soak the beans overnight. The next day, boil until soft and stir into the rice. Other forms of sweetener may be added but these must remain in the background, more like a fragrance; the sweet taste must not dominate:

chopped dried fruits
chopped fresh fruits
chopped crystallized *or* glacé fruits

Tea *(Chá)*

To wake you up – two cups of tea!
CHINESE SAYING, NINTH CENTURY

Tea is a very ancient drink in China, but until the third century AD it was only drunk as a medicine, mixed with other dried herbs or fruits. The tea was made into a solid cake from which pieces could be chipped and then crushed to be mixed with water. During the rise of Chan (Zen) Buddhism in China in the Three Kingdoms period (AD 220–265), tea drinking assumed a more formal and ritualized place. It also came to be appreciated as a beverage in its own right, without the addition of milk or sugar. Mention of the cultivation of tea bushes is found in documents of the fourth century (known as the Er Ya). During the Sui and Tang dynasties (sixth–eighth centuries), tea became a popular drink throughout China, and in 760, Yu Lu wrote a handbook on the tea ceremony which became known as the *Tea Classic*.

Today, tea is the most popular drink in China and hundreds of varieties are available. The main ones are either green or black and many, such as the well-known jasmine tea, have dried flower blossom added to the tea to give special flavour and aroma. The green Longjing ('Dragon Well') tea produced at Hangzhou's West Lake People's Commune is considered one of China's finest varieties. Chrysanthemum tea, an excellent digestive, is also produced in the region.

With the coming of spring, the flavour of tea is at its best. Tea connoisseurs make for the mountains in small groups to make tea with mountain water, for the secret of tea is in the water and spring water is considered the best. The same tea will taste different in different places, because of this variation in water. The water should be brought slowly to the boil and then it should not be allowed to boil long because this will change its flavour. It is not necessary for the kettle or boiling pot to be giving off clouds of steam; rather, watch out for the streams of tiny bubbles which appear when the water is ready for tea-making. These tiny bubbles are known expressively as 'crab's eyes'.

If you come to enjoy your tea the Chinese way, it will be worth keeping some melted winter or spring snow for this purpose. If you ever have access to spring water or a pure mountain stream, take some water home for tea-making. Town water is best left standing for a while to let it 'breathe' before using it for tea.

Tea is prepared in a cup or a pot. Place a teaspoon of leaves in a cup and pour on boiling water. Cover the cup with its lid (if it is a Chinese cup) or a saucer and allow the leaves to settle. Tea is very refreshing when served after a meal or with pastries. When using a pot, put in a teaspoon of leaves per person.

If you have access to a supplier of Chinese teas or have a friend in this position, do not hesitate to enter the world of Chinese tea; it is one of relaxation and delight. Tea is the subtle drink of friends, a comforter in all weathers, an excellent aid to contemplation or to any contemplative art such as reading, writing, looking at natural beauty, drawing, sewing, designing furniture or buildings or meals. It is also the drink of the recluse, the poet, the thinker, the mystic. Yet tea is also the drink of neighbours, a relief in times of shock or bereavement. Among Chinese teas, you will be able to find a tea to suit every mood and occasion.

Wine *(Jiŭ)*

'While I can, I drink the wine in my cup and commend the rest to Heaven's care.'
BO JU YI, 772–846

The Chinese believe that wine is best drunk among good friends, and should be served warm in small porcelain cups. Wine was first presented to Emperor Yu, the founder of the Xia dynasty (2205–1766 BC), but the emperor was wary of its unpleasant effects. The most ancient wines were brewed; later, in the Yuan dynasty (AD 1271–1368), distilled liquor is first recorded.

The dark wines are usually made from fermented glutinous rice. Among these is the famous yellow Shaoxing from Zhejiang province which is aged for at least a year. In former times, jars of Shaoxing would be buried at the birth of a girl child and dug up at the time of her marriage. This matured wine, known as Lao Jiu, would then be used during the celebrations. White wines are usually made from sweet corn and barley, such as the strong Gaoliang Jiu. Another strong wine which has become popular in China, especially for toasting, is Mao Tai Jiu which is fermented and distilled from wheat and millet and in which only the spring water of Mao Tai in Guizhou province, south of Sichuan, may be used. Mao Tai is well aged before being bottled.

China's answer to vodka, Chen Liang Bai Jiu, produced in the north-eastern city of Harbin, is effective in keeping out the cold driving winds which blow there in winter.

Like good tea, a little wine is especially conducive to writing and reading poetry, conversation, to appreciating beauty and music. After a few cups of wine, how easily we can appreciate the poet Li Bo's (701–762) observation: 'I sat drinking and did not notice the twilight.'

Chinese wines have their own characteristic taste. If none is available, substitute dry sherry in the recipes.

Tales of Mu:
The Sound of
Two Persons Laughing

It was not the practice of Lord Wang to spend time among his servants but, gourmet as he was, he could not resist the occasional visit to the kitchen. It always amazed him as he watched his cook, Mu, that no job seemed beneath the man. He seemed as happy cleaning the floor or the cooking pots as he was in preparing a sumptuous banquet.

One day Mu felt himself being observed in this manner and, without ceasing his work, he asked: 'May I be of service to your honour?'

Lord Wang smiled and said: 'Mu, I am fascinated by your equanimity, the harmony I feel in this kitchen. This is why I love to come here.'

Mu bowed respectfully at these words. 'My Lord is always welcome here.'

Wang knew that he was welcome in that kitchen, but he spoke again: 'When I am in this kitchen I feel privileged. I feel more at ease here than I do in the receiving hall. But tell me, Mu, don't you ever feel disgruntled that I am your master, that you are not my equal in society?'

Mu looked up and wiped his hands. 'Your honour has an ancient pot made by a Korean master. Is this not so?'

'Yes,' replied Lord Wang, 'it is my most beautiful pot. I consider it a treasure.'

Mu nodded. 'Just so. What do you keep in this pot, your honour?'

Lord Wang seemed puzzled. 'Why, nothing of course!' Mu reached on a shelf and held out a little brown jar. The cork stopper was sealed with wax. 'This was made by a peasant in the village many years ago, your honour. I have used it continually as a container for pickled vegetables.' Lord Wang thought that he understood Mu's point and he began to chuckle. But Mu continued: 'Which of the two pots – this pot, or the one made by the Korean master – is more of a pot, your honour?'

Lord Wang hesitated. 'Why . . .' He thought he could see a twinkle in Mu's eye.

Thus would anyone happening to be passing by in those days have come to wonder at the sound coming from that kitchen. The sound of two persons laughing.

Notes on Chinese Pronunciation and Pinyin Romanization

The language known today as Chinese is the language of the Han people and has many dialects. Since 1949, the Beijing (Peking) dialect has become the basis of a national dialect and is now spoken by seventy per cent of China's Chinese-speaking population. Outside the People's Republic of China, this dialect is sometimes mistakenly referred to as 'Mandarin'. Inside China, the people call it 'Putonghua' – 'common speech'.

Since 1958, Pinyin ('phonetic transcription') has been the officially endorsed romanization of Chinese, although the West has taken some time to abandon the confusing Wade–Giles system. Pinyin gives a more accurate rendering of spoken Chinese.

The language is tonal – the meaning of each syllable is affected both by the way it is pronounced and by the tone in which it is spoken. This change of meaning is reflected in Chinese writing by a change of character. The four tones are indicated by marks above the vowel:

    ¯ 1st tone, high and level
    ´ 2nd tone, rising
    ˇ 3rd tone, falling-rising
    ` 4th tone, falling

Thus the word *wu* can mean 'house' (*wū*), 'none' (*wú*), 'five' (*wǔ*) or 'fog' (*wù*).

Wherever Chinese words are rendered in italics in this book, tone marks are included to indicate the correct tonal pronunciation. Below is a Pinyin alphabet pronunciation guide:
Pronounce a as the long *a* in *far*

b	as	*b* in *bee*
c	as	*ts* in *bits*
ch	as	*ch* in *chip*, but strongly aspirated
d	as	*d* in *do*
e	as	*e* in *her*

f	as	*f* in *foot*
g	as	*g* in *go*
h	as	*h* in *her*, but strongly aspirated
i	as	*ee* in *meet*
	or	
	as	*e* in *her* in syllables beginning with c, ch, r, sh, z and zh
j	as	*j* in *jump*
k	as	*k* in *kind*, but strongly aspirated
l	as	*l* in *land*
m	as	*m* in *me*
n	as	*n* in *nap*
o	as	*oa* in *board*
p	as	*p* in *park*, but strongly aspirated
q	as	*ch* in *chin*, with the tongue touching the palate
r	as	unrolled English *r* in *right*
s	as	*s* in *sister*
sh	as	*sh* in *shore*
t	as	*t* in *top*, but strongly aspirated
u	as	*oo* in *too*, also like the French *u*
v	as	*v* in *victory* – only in foreign words, national minority words and local dialects
w	as	*w* in *want*
x	as	*sh* in *she*, with the tongue touching the palate
y	as	*y* in *yet*
z	as	*z* in *zero*
zh	as	*s* in *measure* or French *j* in *je*

Glossary

áo braised, stewed
bā eight
báicài Chinese cabbage
báiyóu seasoned with salt
bàn mixture, salad
bāo wrap up
bǎo treasure, delicacy
biǎndòu flat peas, snow peas, mange-touts
bīng iced, crystallized
bǐng cake, biscuit, pancake
bōcài spinach
bōluó pineapple
cài vegetable, dish
càihuā cauliflower
càixīn spring greens, 'hearts of green'
chá tea
chán meditation, Buddhist in the Zen sense
chǎo stir-fry, fry
chénpí tangerine, or tangerine peel; orange or orange peel
chūn spring
cōng onion, green onion, scallion
cū vinegar, sour
dà big
dàshīfu cook, chef
dàn egg
dōng winter
dōnggū dried mushroom (picked in winter)
dòu legume, bean
dòufu bean curd
dòuyá bean sprout
dùn stewed, boiled in its own sauce

fānqié tomato
fānshǔ sweet potato
fàn cooked rice, meal
gān dried
gū fungus, mushroom
gúsuǐ marrow
guì cassia, cinnamon
guǒ fruit
hóng red
hóngshāo red-cooked, cooked in soy sauce
húlóbo carrot
hútáomù walnut
huā flower
huārén peanut
huángguā cucumber
jīdàn chicken's egg
jìdòu green bean, runner bean
jiāng ginger
jiàng sauce
jiàngyóu soy sauce, soya bean
jiāo chilli pepper
jiǔ wine, alcoholic drink
juǎn roll
kǎo baked, roasted
lán blue
láncài broccoli
lìzī chestnut
liáng cold, cool
liù six
lóbō turnip
lóngxūcài asparagus
má sesame
málà hot and spicy
máyóu sesame oil
mǎlíngshǔ potato
měng gū Mongolian

mǐ rice
miàn flour, noodles
mógū mushroom
mù tree, uncarved block
nǎi cream, milk
nánguā pumpkin
ní mashed
piàn slice, flat thin piece
píngguǒ apple
qiézi aubergine, eggplant
qíncài celery
qīngjiāo green pepper
sān three
shāo cooked, baked
shēngsuǐ marrow
shuǐguǒ fruit
sī sliver, shred
sì four
suān sour, pickled
suàn garlic
sǔn bamboo shoots
tān spread out
tāng soup, hot water
táng sugar, sweet
tángcù sweet-and-sour
tián stuffed
tián sweet
tiáo strip, long narrow pieces
tǔdòu potato

wāndòu lima bean, broad bean
wáng king, monarch
wēi cook gently
wěimèi tasty
xiān fresh
xiānmo fresh mushroom
xiāng fragrant, spicy
xiāngjiāo banana
xiāngtáo walnut
xiǎcài pickle, pickled vegetable
xīncài cabbage
xìngrén almond
yàng kind, sort
yǎoguǒ cashew nut
yóu sauce, oil
yú fish
yùmǐ sweet corn, maize
yùshì jade
yuánzi ball, dumpling
yuè moon
yuèbǐng moon cake (especially
  for mid-autumn festival)
zǎo date
zhá deep-fried, fried
zhēnxiū delicacy
zhēng steamed
zhòng masses, the people
zhōu soft rice, congee

Index